· · · · · · · · · · · · · · · ·

INVESTING IN WOMEN:
PROGRESS AND PROSPECTS
FOR THE WORLD BANK

POLICY ESSAY NO. 19

· ·

INVESTING IN WOMEN:

PROGRESS AND PROSPECTS FOR THE WORLD BANK

Mayra Buvinić, Catherine Gwin, and
Lisa M. Bates

Distributed by the Johns Hopkins University Press
Published by the Overseas Development Council in Cooperation
with the International Center for Research on Women
Washington, DC

BHK6569-7/3

Library of Congress Cataloging-In-Publication Data

Buvinić, Mayra
    Investing in women: progress and prospects for the World Bank/Mayra Buvinić, Catherine Gwin, and Lisa M. Bates

Policy Essay No. 19
Includes bibliographic references.
    1. Women in development—Developing countries. 2. Women—Developing countries—Economic conditions. 3. Women—Developing countries—Social conditions. 4. World Bank. I. Gwin, Catherine. II. Bates, Lisa M. III. Title. IV. Series.

HQ1240.5.D44B88   1996   338.9′0083—dc20   96-13453 CIP

ISBN: 1-56517-018-0

Printed in the United States of America

Director of Publications: Christine E. Contee
Publications Editor: Jacqueline Edlund-Braun
Edited by Jenepher Moseley
Cover design: Ripe Studios

Contents

Foreword

How does the world's largest and most influential development institution address the needs of half the world's population? This study seeks to provide some answers to this question by examining World Bank lending that has intended to benefit women, drawing lessons from projects that have apparently succeeded in this respect, and by exploring areas that remain as-yet unrealized opportunities for Bank investments in women.

The quality of life for the average woman in the world has improved notably over the past two decades. However, large numbers of women in developing countries still suffer under conditions of severe poverty, and even larger numbers lag behind men in all social indicators. The 1995 United Nations' Fourth World Conference on Women held in Beijing clearly sent the message to the world that while progress has been made in improving the condition of women, there is still a considerable way to go. The Beijing Conference also revealed a new willingness on the part of governments and other international actors to close the gender gap, a trend that seems to be reinforced by the changes taking place at one of the most influential international actors—the World Bank.

Investing in Women is the product of a joint project of the Overseas Development Council and the International Center for Research on Women that focuses on the role of the World Bank in improving the status of women. Co-authored by ICRW President Mayra Buvinić, ODC Senior Vice President Catherine Gwin, and ODC Program Assistant Lisa Bates, this timely analysis examines the overall record of the World Bank's approach to women in development and gender issues, considers factors contributing to successful projects, and suggests future areas for World Bank action.

Preliminary findings of the project were aired and discussed in the summer of 1995 at a joint ODC/ICRW Conference on the Role of the Multilateral Development Banks in Improving the Status of Women. We are delighted to include, as an appendix to the study, excerpts from the thought-provoking remarks of several of the speakers, who include Nancy Birdsall, Executive Vice President of the Inter-American Development Bank; Margaret Catley-Carlson, President of The Population Council; Mahbub ul Haq, then Special Advisor to the Administrator of the United Nations Development Program; and Sven Sandström, Managing Director of the World Bank.

This nineteenth volume in ODC's Policy Essay series is the latest in ODC's continuing body of work on the international institutions that affect development. Most recently, *Moving to the Market: The World Bank in Transition*, focused on the Bank's role in promoting private-sector development. *Miracle or Design? Lessons from the East Asian Experience* took a critical look at the World Bank's 1993 report on the East Asian "miracle" and the miracle's applicability to others. *Africa Beyond Adjustment* assessed another World Bank report, a 1994 study on the effectiveness of structural adjustment programs in Africa, and offered an alternative perspective.

The Overseas Development Council and the International Center for Research on Women are grateful to The Ford Foundation, the Charles Stewart Mott Foundation, and The Rockefeller Foundation for the support they provided to this project. ODC wishes to acknowledge the generous support of The Ford Foundation and The Rockefeller Foundation for the Council's overall program. The International Center for Research on Women gratefully acknowledges The Ford Foundation for support of its overall program.

John W. Sewell   Mayra Buvinić
President   President
ODC   ICRW

April 1996

Acknowledgments

The authors wish to acknowledge the valuable contributions of Sara B. Newman and Stephanie J. Eglinton, who interviewed Bank staff and worked on various sections of this report. Judith Tendler provided wise guidance in conceptualizing the study. Michael Bamberger, Lynn Bennett, Robert Cassen, Martha Chen, Minh Chau Nguyen, Ishrat Husain, Ann O. Hamilton, Eveline Herfkens, Jan Piercy, Agnes Quisumbing, and Anne Tinker read earlier drafts of the study and gave helpful comments. We are grateful to them, as well as to the World Bank staff who agreed to be interviewed for this study; to the staff at ODC and ICRW who supported our work; and to The Ford Foundation, the Charles Stewart Mott Foundation, and The Rockefeller Foundation who funded this project. The authors are solely responsible for the views in this report.

Executive Summary

INTRODUCTION

■ CULMINATING TWO DECADES OF RESEARCH and advocacy demonstrating important social and economic benefits of investing in women, the 1995 Fourth World Conference on Women in Beijing highlighted the substantial gaps that remain between rhetoric on and action to improve women's lives. While considerable gains have been made over the past 20 years in key social indicators for women, unacceptable disparities in the well-being of women persist and even less has been achieved with regard to women's participation in economic and political life. However, the Beijing Conference also represented a renewed commitment to women's issues in development on the part of a wide array of international actors. The new World Bank president, James D. Wolfensohn, was among those who called forcefully for an end to "empty words" in place of real, concerted action to change the conditions of women worldwide.

As the largest and most influential source of development finance, research, and policy advice, the World Bank has a major role to play in improving the status of women. Women as well as men stand to benefit from the Bank's overall efforts to promote economic growth and reduce poverty. But these measures alone are not sufficient to address the many obstacles to women's full participation in their countries' development. As a result, the Bank has also been engaged over the years in efforts to assist women specifically. A 1995 internal Bank-wide review surveyed the entire portfolio of the Bank and found that 615 out of 4,955 projects from 1967 to 1993 included at least minimal measures to address explicitly the needs of women.

This Policy Essay complements the internal Bank review by 1) examining in-depth and deriving lessons from positive initiatives;

2) highlighting areas of relative neglect on the part of the Bank and drawing attention to these missed opportunities; and 3) identifying a number of cross-cutting issues and further challenges with relevance to all aspects of the Bank's work to benefit women. It is not intended to be an exhaustive analysis of the World Bank's work on behalf of women. The authors' observations and recommendations are based on interviews with Bank staff and reviews of Bank documents concerning selected lending activities. No field evaluation was conducted. While the relevance of macroeconomic and sectoral policy reforms to women's well-being is fully appreciated, the focus here is on *projects*—still the Bank's primary lending vehicle and a major source of policy influence. Similarly, the authors concentrate on projects that reach women with services or resources while recognizing the importance for the well-being of lending that benefits all people, irrespective of their gender.

. . . .

THE WORLD BANK'S RECORD

■   OVER THE YEARS, THE BANK HAS FOLLOWED, not led, analysis and action on women in development (WID) issues. While other donors, particularly the bilateral agencies, have been active since the 1970s, serious momentum in the Bank began in the mid-1980s. Like other donors, the Bank has argued and done significantly more on behalf of women as mothers than as workers. There is in the Bank an intellectual consensus surrounding the importance of investing in women in the social sectors that does not exist with regard to women's roles in economic development. This orientation stems from a disproportionate early emphasis by the Bank (and indeed by development theorists in general) on women's fertility behavior as well as from societal perceptions of women's "natural" roles. The interest in women's reproductive status has led to a number of influential policy statements accompanied by increasing investments in projects benefitting women in population, health, and education. Although there are signs that the institution is moving in the right direction in addressing women's roles in the productive sectors, not enough has been done in terms of operations.

CONCEPTS AND THEIR TRANSLATION

■ THREE CONCEPTS ARE SALIENT in the Bank's current discourse that supports efforts on behalf of women: a shift from "WID" to "gender"; the need to "mainstream" gender issues in operations; and the importance of participatory project lending strategies. All three hold the potential for strengthening investments in women, but in reviewing project experience, this study finds reason to be concerned about the translation of these concepts into practice.

FROM WID TO GENDER

A "gender" approach to development gained popularity after the 1985 international women's conference in Nairobi as a reaction to a prior exclusive focus on women in analysis and practice. Gender emphasizes analyzing inequalities between men and women in the family and in society. In practice, however, the shift from WID to gender in the Bank entails two risks. The first stems from the fact that gender has highlighted sources of inequality inside households. While the focus on intrahousehold sources of gender inequality is desirable, it should not come at the expense of attention to the policy, institutional, and economic bases for women's relative *and* absolute disadvantage. These obstacles are not only pervasive, they are also more amenable to direct intervention. A second risk is that gender will be employed as a more inclusive substitute for rather than as a complement to the WID approach because, as some Bank staff report, gender has the advantage of being more "palatable" to borrowers. However, if this interpretation dilutes explicit attention to women's needs and in fact leads to the diversion of resources to men, it clearly cannot be equated with fulfilling the WID mandates out of which gender was born.

MAINSTREAMING

Along with other development institutions, the Bank is seeking to integrate attention to women into all aspects of its operations. In terms of project lending this entails a shift away from separate WID projects or project components focused exclusively on women. Mainstreaming is indeed a laudable long-term goal, but the Bank's current push for this strategy, based largely on the perceived failings of past stand-alone efforts, will not likely address the underlying causes of these failings. In mainstreamed projects, the focus on women is by definition much more diffuse, and therefore, it requires the assignment of expert staff through-out the project cycle. The Bank has yet to build up a sufficient critical mass of such staff to ensure the success of mainstreaming. Furthermore, as projects reviewed illustrate, targeting women is in some domains essential to project success. As a result, the Bank's present emphasis on mainstreaming may be premature.

PARTICIPATION

Though not born out of an explicit concern for women, "partici-patory" approaches are advocated by many in the Bank as useful tools for identifying and addressing gender issues. Like the gender approach, staff often regard participation as a more inclusive, and therefore more prefer-able, strategy for benefiting women. With heightened awareness of and commitment to the need to reach women specifically, these strategies can indeed be beneficial. However, generic participatory approaches do not automatically ensure the involvement of women and those that do can often be burdensome if they entail substantial contributions of women's voluntary labor. To be successful, projects which entail beneficiary involvement must often take extra measures to remove the obstacles to women's meaningful participation.

At a minimum, clarification of these concepts is required, but in some cases it may also be necessary to slow the pace or alter somewhat these trends until the requisite enabling environment is securely in place.

. . . .

INVESTING IN WOMEN AS MOTHERS

■ HEALTH, POPULATION, AND EDUCATION, as noted above, are the areas in which the Bank has made the greatest strides to address the particular problems of women. This attention comes out of early pre-occupations with women's reproductive roles, but over time these projects have broadened in scope. The approach to women's health has expanded from a focus on safe motherhood to include the health and nutritional needs of women throughout the life cycle, from adolescence through old age. Similarly, projects in population are increasingly addressing the broad range of women's reproductive health needs. And special efforts are being made to target poor women with health services that are not women-specific.

Education is included in this essay among investments in women's reproductive roles because, although the Bank highlights positive effects of girls' schooling on their productivity and future earnings, the rationale for and design of projects primarily underscore social benefits in terms of reduced fertility and maternal and infant mortality, and increased child well-being. Widely embraced across the Bank as central to improving the lives of women and their families, lending for girls' education is one of the most innovative areas of Bank operations. Several Bank projects have employed flexible, experimental approaches to successfully improve girls' access to formal education.

These "bright lights" in the World Bank's lending for women share a number of common features: an intellectual consensus on the issues and the commensurate political will within the Bank as well as the borrowing country; collaboration with other donors or NGOs, particularly women's groups, in the design and implementation of the project; the use of targeting strategies and innovative operational styles; and relatively high representation of women among the professional staff involved. It is also important that these efforts are in sectors where overall lending levels are increasing, which eases competition for resources.

. . . .

INVESTING IN WOMEN AS WORKERS

■ LARGELY DUE TO THE EFFORTS of committed individuals spread throughout the Bank, experiments with measures to better meet the productive needs of women have been undertaken in two areas of lending in the productive sectors, agriculture and financial services. In reaching out to women farmers, the Bank has built on proven strategies and focused primarily on increasing access to extension services. Financial services have concentrated on bringing into the Bank the lessons of microfinance, where well-performing projects outside the modern banking sector (and the domain of traditional World Bank lending) have met the credit needs of poor women. The new multi-donor Consultative Group to Assist the Poorest (CGAP), which the Bank helped launch, is a promising step in this direction.

Two major lessons emerge from the project experience in these sectors. First, the support of Bank management and financial resources is again critical, and perhaps more so than in the social sectors where the rationale and protocol for investing in women is now firmly established. Second, projects that target women and entail a few rather than multiple interventions often yield best results.

Progress in these sectors, however, has been largely piecemeal and in neither agriculture nor financial services is there yet a comprehensive sector strategy for increasing women's participation and productivity. Projects in agricultural extension and microfinance need to be better linked with broader efforts aimed at improving women's access to essential productive inputs and rural infrastructure and at reducing the legal barriers to women's full economic participation.

. . . .
UNREALIZED OPPORTUNITIES

■   IN CERTAIN OTHER AREAS such as infrastructure and compensatory programs, the World Bank has yet to give much explicit attention to how its lending could better include and benefit women.

Still the largest area of Bank lending, infrastructure investments can bring sizeable benefits to women beyond the often cited positive impact of water and sanitation projects on women's home burdens. Infrastructure development raises women's market productivity, opens opportunities to participate in public life, and provides employment. Furthermore, the benefits of other investments in women (e.g., education, emergency obstetric care, agricultural extension) will not be fully realized without accompanying infrastructure development. Yet in neither the 1995 *World Development Report on Infrastructure and Development* nor the 1994 Policy Paper on Women are these links between infrastructure and women's well-being explicitly made. A few pilot schemes have attempted to target women in Bank infrastructure projects, highlighting the importance of addressing access, affordability, and user perspectives in project design and implementation. Overall, the relative neglect of women in this sector represents an important missed opportunity.

Compensatory programs have been in use since the 1970s as a way for governments to transfer income to and protect the poor during economic downturns, often through short-term employment schemes. The Bank, along with other donors, has invested heavily in similar "social funds" as a way of, for example, off-setting the social impacts of structural adjustment. These funds, in contrast to public works programs, have generally failed to provide employment to women (where employment generation is a component of the project) and to adequately involve women and women's groups as fund solicitors and project implementors. Future World Bank investments in this area could significantly increase benefits to poor women by combining the positive features of the centralized public works schemes with those of the demand-driven social funds. They should draw on the public sector's comparative advantage in generating short-term employment quickly, reaching marginalized groups, and collecting the gender-disaggregated data necessary for monitoring progress. Similarly, private-sector involvement in implementation can increase participation and long-term sustainability, promote accountability, and contribute to the institutional growth of nongovernmental organizations (NGOs).

. . . .

CONCLUSIONS

■ A NUMBER OF FINDINGS EMERGE from this review. The Bank's increased work to reduce poverty through projects and policies could go a long way toward improving the welfare of women who constitute some 70 percent of the world's absolute poor. However, these efforts must be attuned to the specific needs of women and must be accompanied by strategies to tackle directly the obstacles they confront. Increasing Bank investments in the social sectors have already brought benefits to women. The challenge now is to expand these efforts while improving their quality and the linkages between projects and policy. In the productive sectors, the commitment to investing in women is more tentative, and there is a pressing need for expanding both quantitatively and qualitatively the Bank's lending for women in these areas. Overall, while the Bank's call to mainstream gender is the right long-term goal, a special emphasis on women and upfront investments is still needed to build up an adequate portfolio of Bank gender lending.

Less straightforward are the lessons for best practice that emerge. Targeting is clearly important in many cases, as the project examples illustrate, but it is not without costs and risks. Self-targeting, where project resources are in theory available to all, but in practice only of interest to the target group, may be a desirable alternative that reduces political and administrative costs. "Minimalist" projects with limited objectives also seem among the most successful efforts, particularly in education, agricultural extension, and microfinance. Although the widespread interest in undertaking integrated approaches is understandable given women's multiple roles and obstacles, it needs to be tempered by a recognition of women's time burdens and technical and institutional constraints. On the other hand, although simple interventions are easier to implement, if treated in isolation of the broader policy and programmatic framework, their impact will be limited.

Also, there are really no choices to be made between policy and project measures nor of working with NGOs as opposed to governments. All avenues must be pursued. Projects often yield direct tangible results, have important demonstration effects, and inform policy decisions. Yet as this essay makes clear, projects are insufficient without broad economy-wide and sectoral policy changes. Identifying and acting on the synergies between policies and projects is an area where the Bank has a significant comparative advantage.

Similarly, NGOs have been critical vehicles for bringing the benefits of development to women, and the Bank's growing involvement with them should continue. Yet there is still a very important role for the public sector to play in improving the status of women. Once again, the Bank is uniquely positioned to play a constructive role by influencing national policies toward women in its dialogue with governments. It is clear that both approaches—reaching out to civil society while providing governments with informed policy guidance—must be employed simultaneously.

Beyond the specifics of project and policy lending, there are a number of institutional steps the Bank could take to help ensure an environment that is conducive to work on behalf of women. These steps to foster an enabling environment include, importantly, the mobilization of additional compelling evidence on the benefits of specific investments in women, expressed management commitment to the goal of improving women's well-being, and the allocation of adequate staff and financial resources to meet the goal.

It is clear from a review of the Bank's lending experience described above that resources and action follow from convincing arguments about the economic payoffs to investing in women and from established best practices based on operational experience. To both help build the "case" as well as guide practice, the Bank should build on its comparative advantage in economics and expand its research efforts, particularly with regard to women in the productive sectors, and do more to disseminate "lessons learned" across sectors and regions.

Staff are also more likely to be convinced if there is a sense that WID/gender is a serious institutional priority that is reflected in the deployment of adequate resources—both human and financial. Prior to the arrival of its new president, there was a perception within the Bank that senior management support for women's issues was waning.

Staff who focus on women's issues in their work have also spoken about the lack of status afforded these efforts within the Bank. Increasing the representation of women on staff, particularly among senior management (as the new president has done recently), can help. However, equally important is the need to remove the stigma associated with this work by reorienting institutional priorities and actively reinforcing staff efforts to reach and benefit women.

At a time of heightened international attention to women's concerns in development, the World Bank has an unprecedented opportunity to actively lead efforts on behalf of women. This essay is written in hope that the new president will build on the commitments he made at the Beijing Conference by embracing these necessary changes and redirecting the Bank's significant intellectual and financial resources in ways that further substantially improve women's contributions to and benefits from development.

Part I
Making the Case for
Investing in Women

INTRODUCTION

■ IN THE INTEREST OF BOTH ECONOMIC EFFICIENCY and social justice, it is time for the international development community—governments, international agencies, and nongovernmental actors—to attend as a matter of priority to improving women's well-being and their participation in public life. Substantial evidence (dimensions of which are cited below) shows that, despite important progress, large numbers of women in many countries live under conditions of severe deprivation. Women in an even larger number of countries still lag far behind men in terms of a wide variety of social, economic, and political measures. Evidence shows that underinvestment in women matters not only to their well-being, but also to the well-being of their families, communities, and countries. Although cultural and social influences explain some of the variations in the roles that men and women play within different countries, the overall quality of life for women varies widely even among countries with shared cultural traditions. The basic well-being of women is not, in other words, a culturally relative concern. Nor is poverty a wholly adequate explanation of inequities between men and women. It is true that much of the severe deprivation of women is found in poor countries or poor communities within countries; and where massive poverty exists, it weighs especially heavily on women. It is notable, however, that levels of female deprivation vary even among countries at the low end of the income scale, suggesting that it is possible to make headway on improving women's lives even in poor societies. Gender must therefore be made an explicit focus of development to deal with the particular obstacles confronting women. This is true despite a significant overlap between poverty-reducing development strategies and the policies and actions required to improve the status of women worldwide.

The Fourth World Conference on Women in Beijing (September 1995) underscored not only the gap that exists between rhetoric about women and action on their behalf; it also revealed a new willingness of nations and international actors to correct this discrepancy. World Bank President James D. Wolfensohn captured well the challenge ahead in his address to the conference: "We at this conference, and the countless millions outside, know that the time for empty words and gimmicks has passed. The time for action is here." This call comes after two decades of research and advocacy that have shown that investing in women will not only redress inequalities between the sexes but also reduce poverty, raise productivity, and accelerate economic growth. It also follows 20 years of clearly insufficient attempts to change the situation of women in developing countries.

ABOUT THIS STUDY

This study is about one important actor, the World Bank, and its potential role in helping to break the cycle of deprivation that engulfs women and advance their economic and social well-being. The analysis examines specific initiatives and projects that have aimed to benefit women in major sectors of World Bank project lending and considers the potential of the Bank—the largest and most influential source of development finance, research, and advisory services—to do even more.

Starting from the point of view that the World Bank can and should work to improve women's lives, the report's core question is *how best* the Bank can contribute to that goal. The key, of course, is what countries and communities are themselves committed to do. The World Bank works best when it is pushing on an open door and operating in partnership with a client. The focus here is on the Bank's role in encouraging and supporting clients' efforts.

The World Bank plays a significant supportive role in many necessary and important ways; but, as the record demonstrates, these actions are not sufficient to substantially improve women's lives. Among the Bank's necessary actions, aimed at accelerating economic growth and reducing poverty, are the pursuit of sound macroeconomic policies and investment in physical and human capital. The World Bank's assistance to countries in these domains is fundamentally important to countries' prospects for improving the well-being of *all* their people—both male and female; likewise, changes in sectoral policies can have significant direct and indirect bearing on opportunities for women as well as men.

But the macroeconomic and sectoral policies needed to promote economic growth and reduce poverty do not fully address the particular problems that block women's opportunities to benefit from their societies' development. Efforts that carry the label "women in development" (WID) or "gender" focus on these particular problems while acknowledging the importance of attaining the necessary condition of stable, noninflationary, broad-based growth. Correspondingly, in assessing the role of the World Bank in improving women's lives, this essay examines the World Bank's own WID or gender policies and conceptual approaches and reviews actions that have been intended to benefit women.

In 1995 the World Bank released a comprehensive internal review of gender issues in Bank operations.[1] Out of 4,955 projects (or 12.4 percent), the review identified 615 projects with at least minimal gender-related actions over a 25-year period—from 1967 to 1993.[2] The review noted that 62 percent of those projects were approved after 1985, when the World Bank became more active in initiating investments in women. It found that attention to women was concentrated in poor countries— over two-thirds of the projects (410) were funded with concessional loans through the International Development Association (IDA)—and in areas of human resource development. The largest percentage of projects was found in human resources (46 percent) followed by agriculture (39 percent). The review concluded that the Bank had made considerable progress in the later years in integrating gender issues into Bank lending, but cautioned that institutional support for gender was fragile and that comprehensive implementation of the Bank's own WID policy awaited commitment from senior management and the assignment of appropriate resources.

This essay complements the Bank review in three ways. First, it examines in more depth selected projects that have aimed to benefit women in major sectors of World Bank lending—spotlighting ones that have seemed to work well and drawing lessons from them. Second, it explores areas that remain as-yet unrealized opportunities for Bank investments in women. Third, the study discusses a number of crosscutting issues that bear importantly on all of the Bank's efforts to improve women's lives.

The study does not attempt an exhaustive evaluation of the World Bank's work on behalf of women, most of which is work in progress, yet to produce definitive results. Its authors interviewed staff and reviewed Bank documents but did not visit projects. While recognizing the potentially large impact of policy and sector analysis and lending, it concentrates on the record of gender-focused project lending. Projects still constitute the Bank's main lending vehicle, influence policy, and offer concrete evidence on actions designed to improve the lives of women. Knowing that conditions vary across regions and among countries within regions, the study does not present a blueprint of what more should be done. Instead, it highlights positive initiatives and points to further challenges that lie ahead in an attempt to encourage a considerable magnification of the World Bank's current investments in women.

. . . .
WOMEN'S STATUS WORLDWIDE

■ CURRENT WORLD BANK INVESTMENTS IN WOMEN are taking place within a context of noticeable but far from adequate improvements in the conditions of women throughout the developing world. There is also considerable flux in thinking about how to extend those improvements to the many women and the many domains of women's lives still being left far behind.

A review of the status of women worldwide reveals several trends.

■ In the 1970–1990 period the quality of life for the average woman in the world improved notably, although with marked differences in the level of this change across regions. Her life expectancy at birth rose by as much as six to ten years in most regions. In 1990 she could expect to live nearly 80 years in industrial countries, and as long as 50 years in Sub-Saharan Africa—an improvement from 47 years in 1970. She had substantially more schooling than she had in 1970, especially in developing countries where the school age population of girls almost doubled in the period. She also had greater access to modern contraception. As a result, over the two decades there was a 40-percent fall in fertility rates globally (see Table 1). Despite this significant progress overall, large numbers of women everywhere still have not participated in these gains. In Sub-Saharan Africa, for instance, more than half of all adult women are still illiterate and their risk of dying in labor or from pregnancy-related causes is several thousand times greater than that of women in industrial countries.[3]

■ In contrast to gains in social measures, there has been less advancement in women's participation in economic life. Progress in the

TABLE 1. FOUR KEY INDICATORS OF WOMEN'S QUALITY OF LIFE

Region	Life Expectancy[a] (years)		Fertility[b] (births per woman)		Girls Enrolled in Primary School[c] (percent)		Women Aged 15–44 Using Modern Contraception (percent)	
	1970	1990	1970	1990	1970	1990	1970	1990
South Asia	49	57	5.8	4.5	53	75	30	39
East Asia	65	72	4.4	2.2	95[d]	113[d]	69	81
Southeast Asia and Oceania	54	63	5.3	3.6	—	—	33	51
Latin America and the Caribbean	64	70	5.0	3.2	89	103	39	52
Sub-Saharan Africa	47	52	6.7	6.5	36	67	14	19
Arab States	57	65	6.1	4.7	46	92	29	52
OECD	75	79	2.1	1.8	104	102	68	73

[a]*Regional average weighted by each country's total female population.*

[b]*Regional average weighted by each country's total female population aged 15–44.*

[c]*Girls aged 6–11. The gross enrollment ratio may exceed 100 if the actual age distribution of pupils goes outside the official school ages, e.g., because of early age at enrollment, repetition of grades, etc. Data for 1970 from UNESCO World Education Report 1991 (Paris: UNESCO, 1991); data for 1990s (1986–1992) from UNICEF, 1995 State of the World's Children (New York: Oxford University Press, 1995); all other data from Wistat Database, Version 3, United Nations, New York.*

[d]*Includes figures for East Asia, Southeast Asia, and Oceania.*

Source: International Center for Research on Women, 1995.

TABLE 2. WOMEN'S SHARE IN THE ECONOMICALLY
ACTIVE POPULATION

(percent)

Region	1970	1990
East Asia	41.2	42.6
Southeast Asia and Oceania	37.6	37.0
South Asia	25.8	22.5
Sub-Saharan Africa	39.8	37.5
Arab States	19.8	20.8
Latin America and the Caribbean	21.7	26.8
OECD	35.1	38.6

Notes: Figures in table reflect women as a percentage of all people 15 years and older defined as being economically active by the ILO. Regional averages are weighted by each country's population.

Sources: Data from Wistat Database; table created by International Center for Research on Women, Washington, DC, 1995.

period 1970–1990, measured by women's rising involvement in the formal labor force, was evident only in Latin America and the Caribbean and in the Organisation for Economic Co-operation and Development (OECD) countries (see Table 2). Women in all developing regions remain engaged primarily in (lower paid) agricultural and informal sector work. Women who have managed to enter the nonagricultural work force tend overwhelmingly to be in low-skilled and, relative to men, lower paid jobs.[4]

■ Improvements in women's well-being have not erased sharp disparities between countries and regions. In the 1990s, for instance, women in OECD countries can expect to live an average of 26 years longer and have four fewer children than women in Sub-Saharan Africa. Progress in social indicators between regions has been uneven, and in some cases the gap in a number of social measures has widened rather than narrowed in the 1980–1990 period. For example, in Sri Lanka the expected fertility rate for women fell from an average of 4 to 2.5 children per woman during the 1980s; in contrast, the expected fertility rate for Afghan women remained at a high average of about 7 children.[5]

■ There is good reason to believe that recent decades have been characterized by a feminization of poverty: 70 percent of individuals living in absolute poverty are believed to be women, and the proportion of rural poor who are women is estimated to have risen from 54 to 60 percent in the 1965–1988 period.[6]

■ Women's economic gains lag behind those of men. The gap between the sexes in economic activity rates was substantial in all regions in 1990. Unemployment data by gender are scanty, but where they do exist, a clear pattern emerges: Unemployment rates among women exceed those among men in every region. There is also a persistent global gap in wages by sex. In the 1990s, for instance, women's wages in manufacturing in 26 countries averaged 74 percent of men's wages in the sector.[7]

■ Gender differences in terms of participation in public life, political status, and rights are even greater. In 1990 women worldwide constituted only 11 percent of membership in parliamentary bodies, no higher than two decades before. Behind women's low participation in political decision making are centuries of legal and social discrimination that national laws and standards in many countries around the world still condone.[8]

■ The one indicator that shows unambiguous gains for women in both absolute and relative terms is education. There have been global systematic gains in closing the gender gap in school participation at all levels. Nevertheless, there is still much to be done: Currently, more than 130 million children who should be attending primary schools are not, and two-thirds of these children are girls.

As Mahbub ul Haq, then special advisor to the administrator of the UNDP, states in his commentary in the appendix of this study: The record to-date is "a story of expanding capabilities and limited opportunities."

. . . .

THE BANK'S OVERALL RECORD

■ HOW HAS THE WORLD BANK addressed the challenges facing women?

For the most part the World Bank has followed, not led, developments in analysis and action on women-in-development issues. In the realm of official development assistance, other donors, most notably specific bilateral agencies, including those of Norway, Sweden, and the United States, took the lead in supporting research and action, especially in the 1970s and early 1980s. This is reflected in the chronology of institutional policy statements. The World Bank issued its first Policy Paper and Operational Directive on gender issues in 1994. The U.S. Agency for International Development (USAID) had issued a similar statement much earlier, in 1982; the Canadian International Development Agency (CIDA) did so in 1984, and the Inter-American Development Bank (IDB) in 1987. The Bank's long public silence on WID issues indicates the low priority management gave to these questions up to the mid-1980s and the years it took for a record and the case for WID to germinate inside the Bank.

The momentum picked up at the Bank in the mid-1980s, when management established a WID Division and appointed WID coordinators in the regions. It is difficult, however, to translate this increased commitment into specific lending amounts and project impacts on women's lives. The official estimate is that 30 percent of projects approved between 1988 and 1994 included *on paper* (not necessarily in implementation) specific gender-related actions, up from less than 10 percent during the preceding decade.[9] The Bank also estimates that it is now lending an average of about $5 billion a year (out of about $21 billion yearly portfolio) for projects that include WID actions.[10] However, the Bank does not track what percentage of this amount supports WID activities. Although these figures inflate the extent of the Bank's work on behalf of women, there is also the possibility of underestimating the work done. The source of undercounting is in other Bank projects that may have benefited women directly without identifying gender specific action in project documents.

Relying on the Bank's internal review and on our assessment of the Bank's gender-related project lending, we conclude that, since the mid-1980s, the Bank (like other donor agencies) has argued and done significantly more on behalf of women as *mothers* than as *workers*.[11] There is intellectual consensus within the institution on the importance of addressing gender in population, health, and education, especially in relation to women's reproductive roles. This consensus does not exist in the productive sectors; despite recent Bank statements to the contrary, we gathered from our interviews with staff of the Bank that they have yet to be convinced of the direct impact on development and on the Bank's own portfolio performance of boosting women's home and market productivity.

The origin of this imbalance or slant in investments is not unique to the Bank and is reflected in the progress women have made in the last two decades—where improvements in capabilities (social indicators) have outperformed improvements in opportunities (economic and political indicators).[12] Early headway in development thinking about women's reproductive roles—in contrast to thinking about their productive responsibilities—has significantly influenced development agencies, including the Bank, and has molded World Bank policy statements and actions. Women's reproductive roles have been more easily embraced in development strategies because of the long-standing concern with population growth; because this preoccupation with rising population numbers has resulted in significant investments in research and generated a valuable body of knowledge on women as reproducers; and because an emphasis on motherhood validates widely held beliefs about women's role in society. In contrast, research on women's productive roles is more recent, and it has yet to generate a similarly comprehensive, empirically derived body of knowledge for both justifying investments and deriving operational know-how. In addition, the focus on women as economic actors is often at odds with prevailing views in donor and recipient countries alike about what women's roles are and should be.

Reflecting these trends, the Bank's most articulate policy statements have emphasized the importance of investing in women because of their reproductive and motherhood functions. They include Barber Conable's 1987 safe motherhood address and Lawrence Summers' 1992 speech on educating women in developing countries.[13] In addition to these speeches, the Bank has made growing investments in women in the expanding sectors of health and education and, more recently, also in population. The Bank's own internal review already cited here confirms this preference in the nature of investments.[14] The Bank has become an articulate and forceful voice in addressing gender questions in these sectors.

Although the record on including women's issues in the productive sectors is more recent and much more tentative, there are signs that the institution is moving in the right direction in addressing the issues of women as economic agents. These signs include the 1994 Policy Paper on Women, the Bank's contribution to the Beijing Conference, which address women's economic roles,[15] and research on gender differentials in agriculture and labor force participation.[16] A specific, concrete indicator of this move has been the recent creation of a multidonor-funded microfinance facility for which the World Bank provides the secretariat.

Despite these advances in attention to women's productive roles, the efforts to-date are uneven, and institution-wide commitment is still lacking. There is too little attention to a coherent strategy that includes linkages between women's productive and reproductive roles and between sector specific efforts—for instance, between education and employment or between credit and extension. The heavy emphasis of the Beijing Women's Conference on microlending as a single or best solution for addressing women's economic needs may exacerbate the problem of undertaking partial initiatives. Also, as revealed in interviews that occurred before the arrival at the Bank of Mr. Wolfensohn, there was a perception among staff that support for gender was waning. The prospects are troublesome since financial pressures on staff to do more lending with fewer resources may seriously jeopardize further investments in women in the productive sectors. In these sectors, there is a less robust foundation of analytic work and operational know-how and, therefore, a need for the type of substantial investments in research and pilot projects that proved critical in the buildup of social sector lending.

· ·

TRANSLATING CONCEPTS INTO PRACTICE

■ THE BANK HAS ENDORSED AND INCORPORATED conceptual shifts in thinking that were articulated first at the 1985 women's conference in Nairobi, Kenya. They include a shift from "WID" to "gender" (and a corresponding emphasis on intrahousehold issues); from separate or stand-alone projects and agencies for women to mainstreaming gender concerns into all operations; and from top-down planning to participatory project strategies. These interrelated concepts are difficult to translate into operations. As a result, we observed inconsistencies and sometimes unanticipated perverse outcomes in the translations of these terms into practice.

GENDER

Some Bank staff argue that the labels "WID" or "gender" make no difference whatsoever in operations. This statement, if accurate, reflects the gap that exists in the Bank (and in other development agencies) between informed discourse on, or rhetoric about, women and weak follow through in operations. But discourse does or should effect action, and it is therefore of concern that the conceptual shift from WID to gender emphasizes *equality* between sexes over strategies to *reduce poverty* among, and open opportunities to, women. Further, by expanding attention in projects to men as well as women, a shift to gender may inadvertently dilute investments designed to remove barriers that specifically confront women.

The WID framework, formulated first by Ester Boserup in 1970, has over time become associated with analysis of women's situation independent of men's and with small-scale women-specific projects.[17] After 1985, WID was replaced in the development discourse with the term gender, in part because WID failed to question economic development models and in part because women-specific projects had failed to improve women's condition. The gender approach calls for assessing women's position relative to that of men and understanding the origins of women's subordination in private as well as in public life. There is, however, considerable confusion about these terms and about their use as a guide to operations.

Gender analysis is an essential tool or method that complements a focus on women—highlighted by the WID approach. However, the gender approach more strongly identifies women's issues in development with inequality between the sexes than does WID. Gender also extends the argument of the origin of this inequality from trends associated with modernization and development interventions to the socially constructed relations between men and women in the family. The gender concept views inequalities between the sexes in public life as derived from and reinforcing inequalities within the family; it therefore moves the focus of analysis from society to the family. Research advances in documenting and understanding the determinants of intrahousehold allocations by sex have provided the conceptual and empirical underpinnings for this shift toward looking at familial sources of inequality.

The Bank's analytical paper for the Beijing Conference identified the household as one of the chief sources of persistent gender inequalities, which are reflected in the market and reinforced by the behavior of public institutions.[18] Emphasizing intrahousehold sources of gender inequality has the twin advantages of demystifying the workings of the household, the former "black box" in development assistance, and of identifying problems within households that are of legitimate concern to policymakers, such as domestic violence or discrimination against female children.

The downside of this emphasis in the discourse is that it underplays policy, institutional, and project sources of gender inequality that are independent of familial origins and that affect the condition of poor women rather than all women. This is not a trivial slant in the discourse because the Bank's overarching goal of reducing world poverty requires specific attention to the condition of poor women. But whether the emphasis is placed on changing household behavior versus changing the way projects, policies, and public institutions affect the well-being of poor women, World Bank analysis is as yet far out-front of its action. So far, there seems to be no clear plan for narrowing the gap between research and action.

The second potential hazard entailed in the shift to gender concerns its interpretation by staff who are either less familiar with the WID/gender discourse or less comfortable with its goals. In theory, the shift to gender requires confronting the root sources of women's subordination to men; in practice gender has taken on a much more apolitical connotation in the Bank and other development institutions. Since gender analysis examines the roles and responsibilities of women relative to those of men, gender has been interpreted as being inclusive rather than exclusive of men. Because of this perception, gender tends to be more palatable to Bank clients and staff than the term WID. Thus, instead of understanding gender as the complementary approach or a tool needed to address women's needs in development, it is viewed by many as a substitute for WID. Indeed, several Bank staff interviewed, uncomfortable with a specific emphasis on women, willingly embraced gender.

However, if gender is accepted because it is believed to reduce controversy over a focus on women, it is not likely to achieve the desired results of enhancing women's participation. In fact, there is some anecdotal evidence that the shift to gender analysis may inadvertently lead to downplaying women's issues in operation. This could occur either by basing the need to target women primarily on their status relative to men (instead of their absolute need) or by diverting scarce resources to issues of concern to men. In the population/reproductive health sector, directing resources to men should help to improve women's well-being since women's sexual and reproductive choices are directly dependent on men's choices. Similarly, promoting greater male responsibility in parenthood is now widely recognized as essential to improving the health and well-being of women as well as children. However, Bank staff interviewed mentioned instances where gender analysis led to investments in boys' schooling in countries where boys drop out of school sooner than girls. Boys catching up to girls in educational opportunities is a worthy development objective in its own right, but should not be equated with fulfilling WID mandates.

At the very least, clarification is needed about these terms and about their use as a guide to operations; but it may also be necessary to reinstate the "WID" orientation in selective areas of operation as a complement to the gender analysis approach.

MAINSTREAMING

Along with other development institutions, the Bank is moving to mainstream attention to women in all aspects of its regular operations: policy dialogue, economic and sector work, and lending programs. In the case of the World Bank and other development agencies, mainstreaming gender has meant incorporating women's issues in sectoral projects as well as in policy initiatives and country programing strategies. In the case of project lending, mainstreaming means in practice that Bank staff are encouraged to integrate attention to women in all aspects of project design and implementation instead of undertaking "stand-alone" projects focused wholly on women or targeting women within larger projects.

The goal of mainstreaming is explicit in the 1994 policy paper on women and was repeatedly voiced by staff interviewed. The recent enthusiasm for mainstreaming is not unique to the Bank, and is also found at other multilateral and bilateral donors. As a means of incorporating WID and gender into the full range of the Bank's work and of encouraging all staff (not just "WID" personnel) to pay attention to women, the Bank's call to mainstream is commendable. However, in practice, mainstreaming entails two main risks.

First, mainstreaming is a reaction to the weaknesses of past stand-alone WID projects and WID components that do not address the causes underlying the weaknesses. Those projects often suffered from government resistance, poor design, inadequate resources, poor supervision, or neglect during implementation. (One staff member reported that she is held accountable for every component of her projects except WID.) Mainstreaming will not necessarily solve these problems; instead, the reasons for the failings of these efforts may yield the same results, if not - worse, in mainstreamed approaches.

Second, WID objectives can be easily ignored in mainstreamed approaches which by their very nature diffuse the focus on women throughout operations. In theory, mainstreaming requires that Bank staff should analyze, diagnose, and design interventions that assist women as part of their regular activities. In practice, WID risks being lost among a stream of concerns—population, poverty, private-sector development, the environment—that Bank staff are directed to address in all sector and country economic work as a matter of priority. Ignoring WID objectives in mainstreaming can be done with relative impunity since this approach makes accountability even more elusive. A recent review by CIDA of its own WID strategy found that integrating gender was a "two-edged sword." Where staff were committed and knowledgeable, it produced meaningful results ; where they were not, it often resulted in mere lip-service.[19]

Mainstreaming can be effective where most staff are knowledgeable and committed, and where funding for actions that benefit women is secure or in place (since mainstreaming WID can add project costs). But the Bank has yet to have a critical mass of such staff and has yet to assign core budgetary resources to implementing WID. Therefore, while mainstreaming should be the long-term goal, all indications are that the Bank is not yet ready to rely wholly on mainstreaming gender in operations. It runs a real risk of losing an emphasis on women in the process. A recent review of mainstreaming gender in three agencies—UNDP, the World Bank, and the ILO—arrives at similar conclusions. It states that the three agencies have not allocated necessary staff expertise and time to mainstreaming and warns that "it would be unfortunate if 'mainstreaming' were used as a cover to avoid committing resources to WID/gender."[20]

Furthermore, as the Bank's recent publications on women acknowledge, there is often a real need to target women when they are overrepresented among the poor and when the gender gaps and barriers are particularly acute.[21] Separate projects or components designed for women should not be abandoned simply because they have been executed poorly in the past. Targeting women with interventions tailored to address the constraints they face was an essential component of many of the success stories that we reviewed, including projects in health, education, and agricultural extension. One exception to the targeting rule is found in population and primary health care projects, where there was no need to target women because they were automatically the primary target group; another exception is well-designed microenterprise interventions whose loans are structured to reach very small borrowers and those working in commerce, a sector where women predominate. In addition, stand-alone WID projects, if well implemented, can have important witness value and usually yield quicker, more visible results. Yet many staff report a real institutional resistance to such types of interventions.

PARTICIPATION

Some Bank staff may not be explicitly concerned about women but nonetheless believe that participatory strategies are good vehicles to address gender and other issues. In contrast to top-down planning, participation and participatory approaches involve clients or beneficiaries in project design and in implementation. Projects that are identified or demanded by clients are sometimes referred to as responding to demand-driven (versus supply-oriented) models. Just as gender may be more palatable than WID to some staff, these broader umbrella approaches to gender also enjoy greater acceptance among many Bank staff who feel that, in the interest of time, money, or fairness, they cannot justify exclusive attention to a single special interest such as women. Paradoxically, however, Bank-led efforts to promote participation and the Bank's sourcebook on participation have paid limited attention to women.

Nevertheless, in the context of using participatory approaches, Bank staff have discovered that women need to be considered in project design and implementation. For instance, in the process of encouraging community participation in the design of community water and sanitation systems in Brazil, a staff member realized that women were the principal stakeholders and therefore their views had to be included to ensure appropriate project design.

There is reason, however, to be careful about efforts to link the Bank's work on women to participation. A broad range of project interventions in the different sectors can and has been designed to benefit women without including participatory processes. Participatory strategies can be costly to women if they translate, as they often do, into women contributing voluntary labor to community-based project activities. Moreover, the project evidence shows that there can be participation without women as often as with women. Community-based associations, such as neighborhood groups or water user associations, and community-based decision making are often hierarchical and exclude women. Even when women are included and are not manipulated by others, they may make inappropriate project choices based on limited, imperfect information, as was pointed out in a recent evaluation of a social investment fund in El Salvador.[22] Projects that use participatory processes need to assess and remove the obstacles to meaningful participation by women.

Against this assessment of the conceptual shifts in the Bank's efforts on behalf of women, we now turn to discuss the experience with project lending, first in the reproductive and related social sectors, then in the productive ones.

Part II
Investing in Women
as Mothers

INTRODUCTION

■   POPULATION, HEALTH, AND EDUCATION are the sectors in which the Bank has made the most systematic efforts to address the particular problems of women. Both public statements made by senior management and increased attention to gender issues in these areas of lending, particularly over the past 5 to 10 years, indicate the Bank's growing commitment. It is these three areas, in other words, that represent the brightest lights in the Bank's growing effort to incorporate special considerations to meet women's needs in the design of its projects.

In part, the impetus for this increased social sector investment in women has derived from a historical concern about population growth and about women in their roles as mothers. This does not mean that initiatives in these areas address women's reproductive roles narrowly or exclusively. To the contrary, important progress has been made in recent years to have a broader impact on women's overall well-being. Projects in population have evolved from a narrow emphasis on fertility regulation in the context of health interventions, to increasingly addressing the broad range of women's reproductive health needs and rights. The attention to women's health started with a focus on safe motherhood but has expanded to include the health and nutritional needs of women throughout the life cycle, including adolescents and older women. And in increasing its emphasis on girls' education, the Bank stresses not only the impact on reduced fertility and maternal and infant mortality, but also the potential positive effect of schooling on girls' future productivity and earnings.

Educational policy and project initiatives, however, have yet to be guided by this more comprehensive rationale, which would argue for stronger emphasis on the quality as well as the quantity of schooling for girls and stress the effects of schooling on female labor market opportunities, among other issues. The absence of this dimension is a missed opportunity in project lending and the reason why education was placed in this rather than the next section of the report.

POPULATION AND HEALTH

■   AS A SIGNIFICANT SHARE of the population currently in need
of greater access to health services, women are likely to benefit substantially from increasing Bank efforts to improve general access to health
services, especially among the poor. But an explicit focus on the particular health problems of women remains necessary. This is because many
women's health issues are unique—more than one-third of the global burden of disease[23] for women aged 15–44 and over one-fifth of that for
women aged 45–59 is caused by conditions that afflict women exclusively
or predominantly[24]—and because their access to health care still tends to
lag that of men.

Since the late 1980s, the Bank has increased markedly its attention to specific health needs of women. Between 1986 and 1993, the World
Bank directed approximately $5.7 billion to over 100 population, health,
and nutrition projects that addressed women's health concerns.[25] The
greater attention to women's health has occurred in the context of overall increases in population, health, and nutrition lending. The number of
new projects approved each year in these sectors increased from an
average of eight in FY1987–89 to twenty-one during FY1990–92.[26]

Historically, attention to women's health within and outside the
Bank has been associated with a concern about fertility and population
growth. Because of the multiple benefits of family planning—to women's
health, fertility regulation, and the prevention of sexually transmitted
diseases and (STDs)/AIDS—that focus is still a major part of interventions targeted at women. But growing awareness of the overall poor status of women's health, the gender-specific barriers to better health, and
the limitations of narrowly defined family planning programs to address
these problems, has led to a more comprehensive approach to women's
health issues.

The case for expanded investments in women's health has been
aided by Bank research. In the early 1990s, Bank staff raised substantial
grant money from outside donors to hold a series of consultations with

women's health experts around the world and to commission several studies on women's health issues and their determinants. In addition to documenting extensively the status of and constraints on women's health, this research supports a rationale for focusing on women's health that is consistent with the Bank's overall justification for investing in women: improving women's health not only promotes equity and improves quality of life, it also has tangible social and economic benefits. Along with women's education and income, women's health is directly linked to child survival and family welfare. Furthermore, nutritional deficiencies, frequent pregnancies, and generally poor health have significant effects on women's productivity, interfering with their ability to maintain a household and/or earn an income. The 1993 *World Development Report* on health has also helped build the case for investing in women's health by highlighting the cost-effectiveness of key women's health interventions.

WORLD BANK LENDING FOR WOMEN'S HEALTH

In addition to their potential for gain from the expanding Bank effort in the health sector overall, women have benefited principally from three interrelated trends in the Bank's health project lending: 1) a widening focus on women-specific health concerns; 2) greater attention to women's needs and reproductive health in population programs; and 3) growing emphasis on poverty-focused primary health care, and within that, attention to poor women's needs.

WOMEN-SPECIFIC HEALTH INTERVENTIONS. An important starting point in the Bank's attention to women-specific health problems was the Safe Motherhood Initiative launched by the World Bank, the World Health Organization, and the United Nations Population Fund (UNFPA) at a conference in Nairobi in 1987. The initiative was born out of concern about persistently high rates of maternal mortality despite impressive reductions in fertility and infant mortality rates.

Since the Nairobi Conference, the Bank has been a leading participant in the safe motherhood effort; has incorporated maternal health issues into its dialogue with countries; funded and conducted analytical work; and supported a number of projects with maternal health components. In FY1986 nine Bank-funded projects with safe motherhood components were under way, compared with over 70 in FY1993. The Bank's substantial involvement in the initiative was largely facilitated by the work of central staff who perceived an opportunity to galvanize attention to a serious women's health issue as well as broader WID themes. Staff concerned about women's health were also able to build support among a broader constituency within the Bank by highlighting the relevance of maternal health to child survival. And at a time when the social impacts of the Bank's adjustment lending were being criticized in broader development circles, Bank management was eager to be publicly supportive.

In practice, safe motherhood efforts both within and outside the Bank have most often taken the form of maternal and child health (MCH) services. However, the proliferation of MCH components in projects can sometimes be misleading; often MCH programs lose sight of the "M" in MCH and/or become overshadowed by family planning/population programs.

Over the years, the scope of the Safe Motherhood Initiative has expanded, although not without debate.[27] For its part, the Bank is still emphasizing maternal health but is increasingly seeking to both address the broader range of women's health issues in its dialogue with borrowers and incorporate interventions beyond maternal health into operations as appropriate. As a result, Bank projects now attend, in varying degrees, to reproductive tract infections, women's overall nutritional status, and other health issues women face throughout their lifetimes. For example, a number of projects, particularly in Latin America, support the early detection and treatment of breast and cervical cancers. And several projects include education components to discourage female circumcision and violence against women.

The Women's Health and Safe Motherhood Project in the Philippines approved in 1995 comes closest to a comprehensive approach to women's health. Its primary objective is to improve the quality and range of women's health services. Among other things, it will support service delivery in maternal care, family planning, diagnosis and treatment of reproductive tract infections including STDs, and detection and treatment of cervical cancer. An important focus of the cancer component is the explicit strategy to shift diagnostic services away from family planning clients to older women, who are obviously more at risk. This is consistent with the goal of addressing women's health needs beyond their reproductive years. The project also has a strong education component that will work with women's groups to advertise services and encourage positive health practices among four specific audiences: "women in unions," (reflecting an attempt, strongly encouraged by the Bank, to expand the focus beyond married women), adolescents, older women, and "special" audiences, such as victims of domestic violence. Another project component supports research on the nature of specific women's health problems such as breast cancer and violence, and on the cost-effectiveness of women's health interventions beyond the essential services. The influence and input of local women's groups, the encouragement and guidance from the Bank, and a visible commitment on the part of the Ministry of Health were all instrumental in achieving the project's comprehensive approach.

FROM POPULATION TO REPRODUCTIVE HEALTH. Although the Bank began lending for population as early as 1968, it has never been a leader in the field in terms of absolute volume, as it provides only about 10 percent of total donor assistance. However, in a number of countries the Bank has been an influential force, shaping policy development and program design, and leveraging additional donor support. Moreover, since the beginning of its lending in this sector, the Bank, more than many other donors, has supported integration of population activities with health and nutrition interventions for both practical and political reasons. Even more recently, the Bank has made the case for an integrated approach to reflect increased concern for women's human rights and general well-being. As a result, much of the approach called for as part of the Bank's population strategy now closely resembles what is being advocated for women's health.

The question now is how to operationalize, in a cost-effective manner, this integrated approach to population. The challenge of translating this conceptual shift into operations is not unique to the Bank; there is very little experience with integrated strategies upon which to draw, and many observers believe that the estimates that emerged from the International Conference on Population and Development of the resource requirements for this broader approach are seriously inadequate.[28] Logistics alone may be a formidable challenge; many existing delivery systems and staff can be easily overloaded if a broader approach is introduced abruptly. Furthermore, preoccupation with high population growth rates, a legitimate concern, will continue to generate pressure to resort to more radical demographically-driven measures until the effectiveness of integrated reproductive health approaches is clearly demonstrated to both governments and donors.

It is difficult to isolate the Bank's influence in this process, since many projects involve multiple donors and, independently, several countries have themselves begun to reorient their programs. Nonetheless, it is notable that some population programs in which the Bank has had a history of lending are showing signs of change and greater attention to gender issues.[29]

PRIMARY HEALTH. In the course of increasing support for health sector projects, the Bank is encouraging and assisting governments to redirect public spending to more cost-effective primary health care, and away from expensive, specialized services and facilities. The recent WDR on health recommends focusing public resources on nationally defined, essential clinical services, targeted largely to the poor, and to public health interventions, leaving health services outside the essential package to private financing. Many of the elements of the essential package outlined in the WDR benefit women equally if not more than men. For example, women benefit disproportionately (either directly or indirectly) from the emphasis on family planning, maternal care, STDs/AIDS prevention, and childhood illnesses.

A Bank-funded health sector support project in Zambia ($537 million with $56 million IDA credit) illustrates the potential benefits to women of a non-women-specific primary health intervention. The project does not include a "WID component" and there is almost no explicit focus on "women"; but it does include efforts to improve the efficiency of the sector and to reorient it to the provision of basic, integrated primary care that includes family planning, pre- and postnatal care, and nutritional supplements. This will have significant positive effects on women who, along with children, are the major users of health care facilities. Moreover, the project has benefited from extensive country-specific analysis with a strong focus on gender issues and from the knowledge of and commitment to women's health of the staff involved. However, because gender issues are integrated throughout, it will, as noted earlier in this essay, be more difficult to trace the project's impact on women, and ongoing monitoring of the project's effects on women will be essential.

Other Bank non-women-specific health interventions have taken explicit measures (usually some form of targeting) to ensure that women's needs are addressed. For example, a population and AIDS control project in Burkina Faso ($34.5 million with $26.3 million IDA credit) reflects an awareness of the high risk women have of contracting HIV/AIDS. Following recognition of the first ten AIDS cases in 1986, a number of studies were conducted to detect prevalence among different groups, revealing alarming increases in infection among pregnant women. Heterosexual transmission accounts for 85 percent of AIDS cases in the country, and a high prevalence of STDs, particularly among commercial sex workers and their clients, greatly increases the risks of HIV transmission. The project seeks to address an insufficient focus on the implications for women of HIV and the unique factors contributing to women's greater vulnerability, such as female circumcision. In order to better reach women, STD/HIV prevention and treatment, including condom promotion, will be integrated with family planning/MCH services. Women will also benefit from national education campaigns against female circumcision and NGO-based education efforts targeted at hard to reach but high risk groups such as adolescents and commercial sex workers.

FUTURE CHALLENGES

Review of the project experience suggests that the World Bank has begun to play a significant role in improving the status of women's health. Gathering and drawing on compelling evidence of the status of women's health, mobilizing external resources, and capitalizing on an efficiency rationale that resonates within the Bank, committed staff have succeeded in galvanizing widespread support for initiatives in women's health within the institution. In turn, the Bank itself has been an effective advocate, leveraging support from other donors and encouraging change in its dialogue with borrowing countries.

A key challenge for the Bank is to sustain the broadened approach to women's health issues in the face of national budget cuts and growing health threats such as AIDS that will increasingly exert pressure on already scarce resources. Until the cost-effectiveness of broader, integrated services for women is better understood, such approaches may be resisted or abandoned in the context of competing pressures. The job for the Bank and its client countries is to see that women's concerns (e.g., in the development of contraceptive technology) are taken into account and that women's access to these health services is maintained or increased. Furthermore, with the bulk of all health care expenditures, including primary health, now in the private sector in most countries, policy efforts have to include improving the quality of private provision and access to it by the poor and poor women. For many of the reasons outlined in the discussion of mainstreaming above, a shift toward overall sector support and away from more narrowly defined health projects will also require vigilance on the part of Bank staff to ensure that attention to women is not lost.

. . . .

EDUCATION

■ INCREASING INVESTMENTS IN EDUCATION is now widely regarded as an, if not the most, important, contribution that international donor institutions can make to improving the lives of women and their families.

As in health, the Bank's rationale for investing in girls' schooling is made on efficiency as well as equity grounds. This rationale has evolved with progress in research. In the 1970s, the Bank expressed a nascent interest in female schooling because of its relationship to delayed age at marriage and reduced fertility.[30] A decade later, the World Bank president singled out expanding girls' schooling as a vehicle to reduce both fertility and maternal mortality rates in developing countries.[31] The simultaneous social and economic benefits of increasing girls' access to education were articulated most clearly in Lawrence Summers' speech in

Islamabad, Pakistan in 1992.[32] Summers estimated the social benefits and the dollar savings—from reduced fertility and infant and maternal mortality—of one additional year of schooling for women in Pakistan and showed the substantial savings that would accrue from investing in this sector. The following year, the Bank's 1993 *World Development Report: Investing in Health,* reinforced this message by singling out investment in schooling for girls as one of the key strategies with largest payoffs in averting deaths and reducing disability in the health sector. And at the 1995 U.N. Conference on Women, James Wolfensohn, in his first major speech as president of the World Bank, proposed a goal of universal primary education for girls and boys by the year 2010. He also proposed that by the same year, boys and girls, in equal proportion approaching 60 percent, should attend secondary school. Toward this goal, Mr. Wolfensohn committed the Bank to increase its investment in education to some $2.5 billion per year over the next five years with a target of 60 percent of that total directed to girls.[33]

PROJECT LENDING

Mr. Wolfensohn's commitment builds on a record of Bank (and other donor agency) project lending that has gained considerable momentum since the mid-1980s. In the 1970s, only 20 of 105 projects in the education sector even acknowledged gender as an issue. In the 1980s instead, 57 out of 115 projects addressed gender inequities and 28 projects included specific actions to reach women.[34] The operational styles of projects that have addressed gender issues in education have, by and large, not followed the traditional World Bank project approach, which involves large loans to government agencies to finance and implement a well-defined set of activities. Operational styles in the education sector better fit a more flexible, learning-by-doing style recently proposed as a more appropriate alternative for social investments than the traditional Bank project cycle.[35] What follows are some examples of approaches being used and of projects that have been important in generating lessons on how to achieve increased girls attendance in schools.

■ *Learning-by-doing.* Girls' education projects have benefited over time from a willingness of project staff to try out interventions and learn from success and failure. A project in Pakistan ($17.2 million project with IDA credit of $10 million) in the early 1980s attempted to increase the number of female teachers by providing rural residences for them. The residences remained unfilled because of social restrictions on women living alone and because the teachers lost their housing allowances if they lived in the residences. Subsequent projects in Pakistan more successfully focused on recruiting and training local women to be teachers. Around the same period, another project in Bangladesh ($52.4 million with $40 million IDA credit) included the provision of free school uniforms in the belief that this would increase girls' school enrollments, which did not happen. Learning from the Bangladesh experience, the government in the Sind region in Pakistan will instead experiment with abolishing required uniforms in rural areas.[36] New approaches are moving away from single interventions to packages that address the multiple constraints and costs of getting girls into schools. The Bangladesh General Education Project ($310.2 million with IDA credit of $159.3 million) has built over 2,000 nonformal and pilot satellite schools closer to girls' homes with the help of nongovernmental organizations (NGOs). The schools have flexible schedules, provide childcare for younger siblings (to reduce opportunity costs of sending girls to school), and recruit female teachers. Textbooks and teacher training methods are being revised to reduce gender bias. Finally, eligible girls at the secondary level receive scholarships for tuition. A midterm review indicated an increase in primary girls' enrollment from 45 percent in 1990 to 54 percent in 1993.[37]

■ *Testing interventions.* Early project designs, which included activities to increase girls' school enrollment rates, did not include collection of gender-disaggregated data, and evaluators were unable to assess project impact. Recent efforts, however, include methodologically sound experimental designs to assess the relative effectiveness of project interventions and evaluate project impact. In the rural area of Balochistan and the capital city of Quetta in Pakistan, some projects provide subsidies in the form of scholarships and education materials to establish private girls' schools. These will be evaluated using an experimental design with randomized treatment and control villages. Baseline and two-year follow-up information will facilitate measurements of changes in enrollment and attendance by sex as well as the effectiveness of private girls' schools on children's literacy and numeracy skills. It will also allow comparisons between government schools and private community girls' schools.[38]

■ *NGOs and communities.* Participation of NGOs and community involvement in design and implementation have been substantial in educational initiatives, have facilitated experimentation, and have reinforced decentralized project management. The project experience has shown that local participation can help alleviate the difficulties of managing decentralized school systems, and local leaders are often willing to bear some of the costs when they are given a stake in the project.

For instance, the Balochistan education project in Pakistan ($330 million with an IDA credit of $106 million) involves communities, parents, and NGOs and brings education down to the most decentralized level in an effort to improve performance, avoid corruption, and ensure accountability. Village education committees of parents are recipients of scholarships and are responsible for recruiting local teachers, overseeing schools, and adding classrooms. A single umbrella NGO implements the school program. This organization disburses funds, subcontracts other NGOs to provide technical support, and monitors technical implementation. By early 1995, 199 rural girls' schools had been created that enroll nearly 78,420 girls. The enrollment rate of girls in these villages averages 87 percent, with several villages reaching 100 percent, compared with an overall enrollment rate for girls in the province of only 15 percent.

■ *Targeting girls.* Most of the World Bank-financed projects that have attempted to increase girls' access to schooling have included an element of targeting. They have varied from recruiting female teachers in Pakistan, to providing scholarships for secondary school girls in Bangladesh, to collecting gender-disaggregated data in evaluations. The project experience suggests that this targeting was a necessary component of efforts to increase girls' access to schooling and reduce the gender gap in education. Targeting alone, however, is not sufficient, and policy and project measures that are universal, that is, that benefit both girls and boys, such as improving school availability and quality, are equally critical to attracting and retaining girls in school.

■ *From projects to policy.* In a review of projects targeted to increasing girls' access to schooling, Elizabeth King and Anne Hill noticed that most efforts began and ended as pilot projects, with short-term funding and implementation support provided by donors and NGOs.[39] Projects have rarely been an integral component of national education plans and have seldom resulted from national education policymaking and planning processes. Yet, policies both in and out-side education affect girls' schooling. Key policy decisions inside the sector include the percentage of national budgets assigned to education and the distribution of that budget. Governments that prefer investing in primary and secondary rather than tertiary schooling will by defini-tion benefit girls more because they are more likely than boys to quit school at earlier levels. There is also evidence that improvements in both availability and quality of primary schools, especially in rural areas, can have a larger impact on girls' when compared with boys' schooling attendance. Other evidence has emerged that quantity and quality are more often complementary than subject to trade-off.[40] Important policies outside the educational sector that increase girls' access to schooling concern basic investments in rural infrastructure, including roads and transportation that can help families overcome obstacles to sending girls to school and employment policies designed to increase women's economic opportunities, among others. But often pub-lic policies are difficult to change or to implement (many stay in the books) while projects can be effective bottom-up mechanisms for chang-ing policies; and there is evidence that this is happening with girls' education projects.

An education sector project in Gambia ($21.2 million with $14.6 million IDA credit) included a component in the design to improve female enrollment and retention rates. Through the efforts of a committed staff member, the gender component, which had not been immediately imple-mented, was activated and included the development of gender-sensitive textbooks and increases in the number of females in teacher training courses. Community-based research was undertaken on the perceived obstacles to sending girls to school (financial costs and sexual harass-ment) and this process was useful in generating community involvement in the project. Policy changes that resulted from this project included lowering the entry age for school children and modifying the criteria for teacher training.

Studies in the Balochistan project found that as many as one-third of students enrolled at boys' schools (segregated by government regulation) were girls. The project, therefore, included a policy condition that the government agree that schools be coeducational, which helped to legitimize girls' participation in schooling. Another policy condition was the reorganization of the Department of Education and the addition of a Directorate of Primary Education to place more attention on primary education and help the government shift priorities to primary schooling. A follow-up Bank-funded 1993 social action program in Pakistan assisted the government in shifting allocations to primary education and in setting goals for girls' school enrollments. Policy changes grounded in project interventions, like the above, have greater probability of successful implementation.

. . . .

COMMON FEATURES IN
SOCIAL-SECTOR PROJECTS

■ SIX COMMON FEATURES we identified in the projects reviewed in health, population, and education that seem to have facilitated the incorporation of gender concerns into project lending include the following:

■ First is the intellectual consensus within and outside the Bank that attending to women's needs in these areas is relevant for development. This consensus exists as well in the borrowing countries and is due at least in part to the availability of research that makes the case for investing in women in terms of efficiency rather than equity. At the operational level, staff emphasize the importance of having fertile ground in borrowing countries to undertake these interventions.

■ Second, many of these projects involve multiple donors and are good examples of collaboration between donors as well as between donors and women advocates in the nongovernmental sector. In fact, it is often as difficult to isolate the Bank's influence in some of these projects as it is difficult to isolate the influence of other donors. In part this can reflect the few monies allocated to WID/gender in donor agencies, which requires donors to combine their resources; and in part it can reflect the uphill battle that still exists in persuading borrowing countries of the benefits of investing in women, with the result that there tends to be multiple donor funding of the few visible star projects or activities. Although both these factors may be at play, donor collaboration has in fact shown the importance of alliances in implementing gender projects. Bank staff in health and population have been effective in developing alliances with women advocates who have pushed for gender issues in national and international fora, such as the 1994 U.N. International Conference on Population and Development (ICPD) Conference in Cairo.

■ Third, participation of NGOs, either in advocacy or in implementation, is often substantial in these projects, particularly in comparison with regular Bank operations where the government is both client and implementor. The participation of NGOs in project implementation carries (among other things) the liability of restricted project coverage but includes the advantages of being able to reach women clients more easily than the government and to accommodate more flexible implementation styles. NGOs, especially women-based NGOs, have been far ahead of governments in terms of implementing WID/gender action, so it is not surprising that Bank projects that benefit women use nongovernmental agencies for implementation.[41]

■ Fourth, targeting women with specific interventions is a feature most projects have in common.

■ Fifth, projects in health and education are among the fastest growing areas of World Bank lending, having tripled in size under Lewis Preston's presidency. This means that they are endorsed by management and that, at least in theory, they face comparatively less competition for scarce resources. However, staff who have worked on these projects have also been successful in securing substantial outside funding, in the form of trust funds, to finance research and other activities associated with project development and implementation. This means that in reality monies to do WID/gender work are still scarce, even in expanding World Bank lending areas.

■ The sixth and last common element is that these projects are in sectors where there is more representation of women among the professional staff.[42] Many staff feel strongly that this has been a key factor in increasing a focus on women in operations.

Part III
Investing in Women
as Workers

INTRODUCTION

■ AS NOTED ABOVE, THIS STUDY finds that overall the record of the Bank (and other donors) on addressing the particular problems confronting women is weaker in the productive than in the social sectors. This finding in no way overlooks the fact that Bank support for macroeconomic and sector policy changes has substantial implications for improving the well-being of both men and women. However, even studies undertaken within the Bank have made the point that "the absence of attention to gender in upstream macroeconomic analysis and policy formulation ... [constitutes] a systemic obstacle to promoting gender-responsive development."[43] Moreover, project lending, on which this study has concentrated, underscores the primacy the Bank has given to increasing women's access to population, health, and primary education when compared with expanding their economic opportunities. Access to these social services is, itself, an important enabling condition for improving the economic well-being of women, but other barriers to productive work remain inadequately addressed.

Certain specific efforts in the fields of agriculture and financial services represent positive exceptions to this general record. In the cases of both agriculture and credit, a combination of supportive, largely external, research and experience as well as the efforts of determined Bank staff have provided the major impetus to the actions to-date. But even in agriculture and credit, the Bank has yet to develop comprehensive strategies for reducing biases against women and for increasing women's productivity.

AGRICULTURE

■ LENDING FOR AGRICULTURE has declined as a share of total Bank lending from a peak of approximately 30 percent in 1978 to 14 percent in 1993. The Bank attributes much of this trend to major decreases in lending for poorly performing types of investments, particularly integrated rural development projects. Despite this steady decline, the Bank still provides 30 percent of all agricultural assistance to the low-income countries of Asia, Africa, and Latin America.[44] Attention to women in Bank agricultural lending is most apparent in Africa and Asia, where 75 percent of the world's poor reside.[45]

The Bank's attention to women in agriculture builds on a long-held understanding that women play critical roles in food production and increasing roles in cash-crop production in developing countries. It is also well known that they achieve this despite unequal access to land and water, to inputs such as improved seeds and fertilizer, and to information.[46]

In addition to supporting macroeconomic and agricultural sector policy reforms intended to benefit both men and women farmers, one of the Bank's main approaches to helping women farmers directly is to encourage the provision of farm extension services to them. This effort reflects a considerable body of research showing female farmers typically lacking access to agricultural extension that can significantly improve their farm productivity. Early efforts to target women with extension had a primarily welfare orientation, consisting of parallel but separate extension services that offered women farmers education in home economics subjects such as hygiene, nutrition, child care, and sewing. More recent efforts have tried to bring women into mainstream agriculture activity by making both quantitative and qualitative changes in extension services.

TWO APPROACHES FOR EXTENSION FOR WOMEN

Two Bank projects—the Women in Agriculture program in Nigeria and the Gambia WID project—illustrate different approaches for extension for women. The first recruited female extension agents, the second reoriented extension services to female farmers. Both projects have performed well and have benefited from the fact that developing extension services is something that the Bank knows how to do and does well.[47]

NIGERIA'S WOMEN IN AGRICULTURE PROGRAM. The Women in Agriculture (WIA) program in Nigeria was launched in the late 1980s. It was a response to the interest of Bank staff working on agriculture in Sub-Saharan Africa and the availability of external (UNDP) funds that were used to generate operationally relevant information on women's work in farming systems in four African countries. Compelling findings showed women responsible for as much as 70 percent of all farm work yet largely neglected in existing projects. Armed with this information, Bank staff convinced the Nigerian government of the efficiency of redesigning its Bank-funded agricultural extension program to better reach women farmers by training a cadre of female extensionists. This objective coincided with the Bank's agricultural lending to Nigeria at the time that called for substantial expansion in extension services and in the number of extensionists trained.

Several operational features appear to have been important to the project's success in reaching its intended female beneficiaries. Using UNDP funds to cover early pilot activities, the project redeployed female home economics extension agents already working for the government into state agricultural units and gave these female agents intensive training in agriculture and extension methodology. To strengthen institutional capacity, a full-time female Nigerian agriculturalist was hired in the Bank's resident mission, and each of the implementing agricultural units was provided with a full-time woman agriculture coordinator. To encourage staff participation and commitment, the program also adopted an incentive system giving female staff slightly higher pay than their male counterparts and transportation and medical allowances. Although some of these actions added project costs, the redeployment of existing extensionists rather than the recruitment of new ones that would otherwise have been required by the expansion, resulted in considerable overall project savings.

The program's single-purpose, focused objective of increasing women's access to extension seems also to have contributed to its successful implementation. The participation of local women and built-in flexibility helped to make the program responsive to specific local needs. In states without adequate numbers of qualified female staff, women extensionists were used to introduce male agents to female farmers and male agents were trained to better reach women by, for example, meeting with them in groups. In the northern states, where purdah predominates, the program spent additional preparatory time organizing women's groups and having informational meetings with men to overcome cultural constraints.

In 18 months, the number of female agriculture extension agents doubled and the number of female farmers in contact with services tripled. Because impact studies have not yet been done, the program's effect on women's productivity is not yet known. However, one observed trend since its inception has been the increased adoption of improved cassava varieties. Since about half of the production and all the subsistence processing of cassava is done by female farmers, it is likely that the use of female extensionists facilitated adoption. The Bank, with help from Nigerian female staff, is piloting similar programs in Malawi and Ghana.

GAMBIA'S WOMEN IN DEVELOPMENT PROJECT. In response to past Bank agricultural investments flowing exclusively to traditional male-cultivated crops, the Bank developed a multi-sector stand-alone WID project (a $15.1 million project with $7.0 million IDA credit) to increase women's productivity. This focused particularly on horticulture and livestock, through better extension, access to inputs, and increased savings. Unlike Nigeria, Gambia had no pool of existing female extension staff available for retraining. Instead, the project purchased the services of several extension units in the Ministry of Agriculture to target female farmers.

Within two years (between 1989 and 1991) women's participation in extension activities increased from 5 percent to 68 percent of all contact farmers. Evaluations of the project have found a significant improvement in women's knowledge, but again, it remains to be seen if this greater awareness will translate into increased productivity.

Free-standing WID projects are rare in the Bank, and staff had to push internally to get the Gambia project accepted. But staff report that the visibility of and substantial resources allocated to this stand-alone effort were key to generating government support and commitment as well as overall project success.

Agricultural extension is, in other words, an area in which the conventional wisdom holds that there are good economic reasons to give special consideration to the needs of women. As the examples just mentioned reveal, the Bank can successfully train female extensionists and deliver extension to women farmers and has the potential to spread these practices widely.

As extension practices targeted to women farmers are spread, the Bank can play a leading role in helping to produce more knowledge on the effectiveness of different approaches to determine, for example, if and when female extensionists are crucial. Knowledge is also needed on how to improve the quality, not just the availability of the extension services and how to increase access to extension for female farmers engaged in tradable crops. Extension, itself, is of course not enough to raise women's farm productivity. Indeed, the success of extension services will depend on an array of additional measures—in agriculture and beyond.

There are some innovative projects within the Bank that aim to improve female farmers' access to necessary agricultural inputs in addition to extension. These include, in the short term, increased access to water, fertilizer, seeds, and credit and more secure access or title to arable land and, in the medium term, improved rural infrastructure (especially roads). For example, the Small Farmer Services Project in Chile ($95 million Bank loan) is taking steps to simplify and encourage land titling for female heads of households. Similarly, various states involved in the India National Sericulture Project are experimenting with different approaches to ensure women sericulturalists access to land, either individually or in groups. And both projects are also adopting innovative methods of getting women access to credit.

However, agricultural sector innovations to benefit female farmers beyond extension services are still too few. Despite an abundance of anecdotal and piecemeal evidence on the extent of women's participation in agriculture, female farmers are still largely "invisible" in the sector. The lack of reliable data on women's agricultural contributions and on the increasing feminization of agriculture has serious implications for operational success. Moreover, what is really needed by the large numbers of poor women farmers is the essential package of the necessary agricultural sector measures, combined with policy reforms in the sector, within a stable macroeconomic environment.

. . . .

CREDIT

■ IT IS WELL KNOWN that there are serious imperfections in credit markets that, along with other obstacles, impede access of small-scale borrowers, including both men and women, to credit and other financial services. In the past, much World Bank lending to local financial intermediaries has gone to government-owned development finance corporations that have issued a majority of loans to medium and large rather than small-scale farms and firms.[48] As primarily small-scale producers and microentrepreneurs, in need of small, short-term loans for working capital rather than for fixed assets, women in developing countries have had little access to these Bank-supported financial intermediaries. Instead, microfinance agencies in the nongovernmental sector have provided these women with access to credit outside the formal banking sector, the domain of most World Bank lending in financial operations.

In recent years, however, some World Bank lending has sought explicitly to benefit women entrepreneurs. The number of such project loans grew after 1988, and by 1991 amounted to an investment of approximately $226 million in loans and grants from the Bank and other donors, which the Bank administered. Loans targeted small entrepreneurs but seldom applied the minimalist "best practices" techniques embedded in microfinance that call for the provision of financial services (credit and increasingly savings) and little else.[49] Instead, loans often featured integrated packages of financial services combined with training and/or training and technical assistance without credit.[50]

For instance, World Bank WID projects in such countries as Gambia and the Ivory Coast have focused more on training than on the provision of credit, with small loans used as sweeteners for training programs. Typically, project administration is in a government's women's ministry, which receives a special budget allocation for the project. The ministry sets up a project management unit and trains staff who, in turn, train rural women in a range of skills (from hygiene to basic business skills). When rural women complete their training, they are offered start-up funds to launch their own businesses.[51] Unfortunately, designs like these are more often than not recipes for disaster. Two decades of experience with income-generation projects for women shows that these designs fail in generating income for women because they overtax the implementing agency. They also overburden poor women by, among other things, offering more than one service (training and credit); emphasizing training in different skills, many of which are assumed wrongly to be easily learned by poor women because they have been identified as traditional female skills (like sewing and embroidery); and using agencies that do not have the necessary technical expertise.[52]

THE SUCCESS OF MICROFINANCE

The gender-related success of microfinance operations is measured in terms of access, performance, and benefits. First, in contrast to the restricted access women small borrowers have had to formal financial services, they have become the majority of clients in most microfinance portfolios. Microfinance agencies have provided reliable access to credit and saving options to more than 3 million women small borrowers in developing countries.[53] The success in access is no mystery. There is a long tradition of women and the poor using informal mechanisms to both borrow and save. Microfinance has been able to replicate the attractive features of informal sector lending to attract women clients (small loans, no paper work, no investment restrictions, and no traditional collateral requirements) while at the same time minimizing the risks associated with informal lending.

Microfinance agencies have increased access by targeting women clients, both directly and indirectly. Some institutions explicitly target women by having credit lines only or mostly for women (Women's World Banking and its affiliates around the world); including a target percentage of women to be reached, allocating a portion of the portfolio to be disbursed to women, and providing staff incentives to reach women [Programa de Desarrollo de la Microempresa (PRODEM), the ACCION affiliate, in Ecuador]; or hiring female credit extensionists (the Women's Entrepreneurship Program in Bangladesh). Others make no explicit distinction between male and female operated enterprises but indirectly target women by the way the loan and saving portfolios are structured. Or they target sectors, such as commerce, where women predominate as microentrepreneurs (Banco Sol in Bolivia; PROPESA, the ACCION affiliate in Chile). In addition, most of these institutions routinely disaggregate and monitor the loan portfolio by gender, a practice that contributes significantly to expanding outreach to women.

Second, microfinance institutions have on average performed admirably well. They provide women with access to a critical resource to increase their productivity, reliably and at low cost, both in terms of direct and opportunity costs. This stands in contrast to the typical income generation project for poor women that demands considerable volunteer time from project participants. The best performing microfinance agencies charge positive interest rates, exhibit very low arrears, mobilize savings, and, as the volume of operations increases, build up financial efficiency and reduced subsidies.[54] Last, the benefits to women producers and entrepreneurs can be both direct and indirect. Women build a credit history. The evidence for programs in Latin America and the Caribbean shows that credit can increase the profits of women-based enterprises, ranging between 25 percent in some programs and 50–100 percent in others.[55]

But microcredit is no panacea for low-income women and the enterprises they operate. The small size and low technology that characterizes most women-operated or -owned enterprises and, therefore, the small amounts women borrow and save, make it difficult for microfinance programs to graduate women clients to the formal financial sector; thus, it is hard for credit alone to upgrade or transform women's enterprises. Women-owned or -operated enterprises often function in policy environments that are hostile to their promotion and growth; these hostile environments are characterized by policies in the financial sector (such as interest rate subsidies and collateral requirements) that benefit large over small borrowers. Other policy constraints that hinder women entrepreneurs include business regulations and property laws—problems that World Bank financial sector loans are increasingly trying to address.

Although past Bank efforts have been disappointing from the perspective of benefits to women, recent Bank initiatives in the broad area of financial sector reform open up opportunities to significantly increase benefits to women. These initiatives include a growing internal movement to bring into the institution the best practices of microfinance lending programs and expand the Bank's financial lending portfolio in this area.

First, and foremost, the Bank's current efforts in promoting financial sector reform can help to provide the appropriate policy environment to increase women's access to formal financial services. But this access depends as well on changes that bring into commercial banking institutional features from microfinance that increase women's access to credit and savings. Such features include reduced collateral and application requirements and diversification of bank branches into low-income neighborhoods. The Asia region Gender and Poverty (GAP) team is working to bring the experience and best practices of microfinance into the Bank and develop operational models and guidelines that task managers can use to design appropriate financial services for women. The team has launched a program of best practices research to document the successes of microfinance projects and derive lessons to replicate this success within World Bank operations. Conditions that have helped the team undertake this work have included the following: longstanding, innovative efforts emanating from within the region itself, support from management in the Asia division, and trust fund monies that have been sizable and covered more than 80 percent of the team's work.

Most recently, the World Bank, together with other donors, has launched an initiative to provide more than $200 million in loans and grants to institutions that provide financial services to the very poor. The new Consultative Group to Assist the Poorest (CGAP) was in part the result of a Bank-hosted International Conference on Actions to Reduce Global Hunger (1993) that NGOs urged the Bank to convene. With a World Bank contribution of $30 million and additional amounts from other international and bilateral donor agencies, CGAP has been established to derive lessons learned and to provide grants or loans on a matching basis to microfinance institutions that assist the economically active poor—including for ongoing and planned Bank operations involving income and job creation among the poor. A novel feature of this new facility is its Policy Advisory Group, which involves key leaders of microfinance programs, including a number of women leaders.

An objective of the CGAP is to channel lessons from the CGAP portfolio into Bank's practices, further improving Bank's lending in microenterprise finance and development. Another is to enable "very poor men and women to become progressively more productive," with the expectation that some participants will graduate to the formal banking sector. The future of main World Bank work appropriately lies with what to do in financial sectors more broadly, including policy and institutional reforms that will gain women access to commercial banks, increase the likelihood that men and women micro-borrowers can graduate into the formal banking system, and make credit available to dynamic small- and medium-sized businesses that have the capacity to generate employment opportunities through growth. At the Women's World Banking Global Policy Forum in 1995, finance ministers, leaders of commercial and development banks, international organizations, entrepreneurs, and microenterprise lenders concluded: "The goal should be to . . . encourage the development of sound, responsive financial retail institutions that serve the majority."[56]

Much of this challenge still lies ahead.

. . . .

COMMON PROJECT FEATURES

■   TWO THEMES OR CONDITIONS already mentioned for health, population, and education emerge again for the set of projects examined in areas of agricultural extension and credit, underscoring their importance. First, the support of Bank management and financial resources both from within and outside the Bank were critical (and perhaps more so than in the social sectors) for launching activities that benefited women in agricultural extension and financial services. Second, targeting women was an important element in these projects. Both cases also underscore a tried but true lesson that projects focusing on few, well-known rather than multiple interventions are more easy to implement and more successful. The Nigeria agricultural extension program trained female and male extensionists and did nothing else. Minimalism is one of the key elements in the design of microfinance operations, and most of these projects have an admirable record in terms of reaching women borrowers. But neither area of activity can bring long-term gains without efforts in related areas such as infrastructure and institutional development and removal of legal barriers to women's full economic participation.

The project review also showed that in neither agriculture nor financial sector lending is there yet a comprehensive sector strategy for increasing women's participation and productivity.

Part IV
Unrealized Opportunities

....
INTRODUCTION

■   IN OTHER AREAS, INCLUDING INFRASTRUCTURE and compensatory programs, the World Bank has yet to give deliberate attention
to how its lending could better reach and benefit women. Despite some
research and operational experience that highlight gender dimensions of
lending in these domains, the special needs of and impacts on women have
been largely neglected. A few (relatively new) Bank projects in these
areas address gender issues to some extent, but there are a number of
ways in which both project performance and the benefits to women could
be significantly improved. These areas present important opportunities
for increasing women's productivity and reducing their poverty through
World Bank lending.

....
INFRASTRUCTURE

■   INFRASTRUCTURE SERVICES—including power, transport,
telecommunications, provision of water and sanitation, and waste dis-
posal—are central to economic growth and to improvements in standards
of living. Typically, provision of these services tends to be highly capital
intensive. For both these reasons, and in the absence of available private
capital, infrastructure development has always been the Bank's largest
area of lending. Although down from a level of 75 percent of total lending
in 1960, it still accounted for as much as 40 percent in 1994. In absolute
terms, Bank infrastructure lending has increased nearly every year since
1960. This mirrors the fact that infrastructure typically represents about
20 percent of total investment, and 40–60 percent of public investment in
developing countries.

   As detailed in the World Bank's 1994 *World Development Report:
Infrastructure for Development*, investment in infrastructure services
has essential links to increases in economic productivity and contributes
to poverty alleviation. These connections occur both indirectly through

greater productivity and expanded employment opportunity and directly through improvements in such living conditions as safe water and sanitation facilities. Nevertheless, despite its centrality to the Bank's activities and improved well-being, infrastructure has not been an area of focus in the design of strategies to overcome impediments to women's participation in and benefits from development. Nor is infrastructure development identified as a priority issue in the Bank's Policy Paper on Women (1994). Frequent mention is made of specific ways in which lack of adequate infrastructure impedes improvements in women lives. For example, it is noted that poor roads and limited public transportation hinder rural women from receiving teacher training; not having a school within easy reach of home is a more important barrier to girls' enrollment in school than to boys'; and lack of quick access to clinical facilities contributes to high rates of maternal mortality due to complications from pregnancy. But provision of infrastructure services and employment of women in that process is not included in the list of key policy actions. Not surprisingly, gender issues are mentioned only in passing in the 1994 *World Development Report* on infrastructure. The report acknowledges gender-specific effects of basic infrastructure linked to poverty reduction and the importance of credit to women to pay the up-front costs of connection to public services. But it gives no gender-specific policy guidelines or prescriptions. This lack of emphasis on the role of infrastructure development in improving the well-being of women is a major missed opportunity.

BENEFITS TO WOMEN

The literature on women in development, beginning with the early writings of Ester Boserup and Irene Tinker, among others, has tended to focus on the potential negative impacts on women of infrastructure projects; their positive implications as means to improve women's well-being and economic condition have received less attention.[57] But sizable benefits to women of infrastructure investment can result in benefits to women that extend well beyond the often cited impact of water and sanitation projects in reducing women's home work burdens. Indeed, the payoffs on other investments in women (e.g., schooling, agricultural extension) will be constrained without accompanying infrastructure development.

There are at least four specific ways that infrastructure investment can benefit women: reducing women's work burdens; raising their productivity; opening opportunities to participate in public life; and providing employment. First, the right kind of infrastructure investment reduces women's burdens from reproductive and home production responsibilities. The benefits are both direct and indirect. Access to clean water and sanitation, rural roads, and electricity directly improves women's health and reduces the time women spend in home production activities collecting water and fuelwood and disposing of waste. In addition, by reducing infant mortality and family morbidity, infrastructure investments reduce the physical and psychological costs of child bearing, fertility, and the time women devote to caring for sick family members. Lack of access to health facilities, especially in emergencies, has been identified as the most critical failing in the maternal health system.[58] Access to potable water explained the sizeable drop in infant mortality rates in Chile during the mid-1970s.[59]

Second, investments in roads and irrigation, other transport, and electricity lowers production costs and raises the productivity of women's market work on and off the farm, in the firm, and at home. Households' access to reliable public utilities has a larger impact on women's market productivity simply because women, more so than men, use and have always used the home as a preferred workplace. The importance of home-based market work for women has expanded with export firms' reliance on piece work and subcontracting arrangements with small informal sector producers.[60]

Third, economic infrastructure can open doors to public life and increase women's access to economic and social opportunities. Because of social and cultural restrictions to women's physical mobility, present in different degrees and forms in all societies, safe roads, reliable transport, and well-lit streets, among other things, can open girls' and women's access to schools, markets, and jobs outside the home. These beneficial effects should be greater for women than for men. An often quoted World Bank analysis estimates that rural road investment could increase girls' school attendance in Morocco by 40 percent.[61] Last, infrastructure investments can provide women with access to the labor market by providing them with employment in public works programs (see next section). Such infrastructure investment adequately designed to benefit women could have a significant impact, not only in reducing gender gaps, but also in narrowing the sharp disparities observed in social indicators between better-off and less-well-off women between and within countries.

CONDITIONS FOR SUCCESS

The features of access, affordability, and user perspective need to be considered to improve both benefits to women and the performance of infrastructure investments. Most of the women (and men) who do not reap the benefits of infrastructure are poor. Poor women's low access to infrastructure services is the first hurdle that needs to be overcome to enhance these investments' gender-friendliness. Government policies that assign priority to infrastructure, that benefit poor households, and that subsidize access to public infrastructure services by the poor are key. This does not necessarily mean public provision of infrastructure, but it does mean sectoral policies giving attention to infrastructure that will benefit poor women and provide realistic options for the poor to have access to services.

The second feature, that rises in importance as public services are being privatized and cost recovery schemes are gaining in popularity, is poor women's capacity to pay for these services. Raising women's productivity is directly linked with increasing women's capacity to pay for service options that they have access to, and poses a typical quandary in development work: Price subsidies of basic services have often benefited the rich, while cost recovery assumes capacity to pay that, especially in the case of poor women, is dependent on their ability to use those same services. Credit and targeted subsidies need to be developed to unlock this typical access and affordability dilemma.

The experience of an innovative pilot scheme included in a World Bank infrastructure loan to Ghana shows the constraints women have in paying for services. A $96 million World Bank loan to support road and railway rehabilitation, trunk road stabilization, and institutional strengthening for transport sector agencies in Ghana included a $2.9 million pilot scheme to test a women-targeted poverty alleviation approach on a feeder road project. Among other interventions directed to women, including providing them with paid work, the pilot offered cycle trailers to reduce women's head loading burdens. The effort was unsuccessful because women did not own and could not afford to buy the bicycles needed to pull the trailers.

The problem of affordability for women is often compounded when volunteer labor is used as a mechanism to recover costs of building or maintaining systems. Participatory approaches are increasingly common, especially in rural water and sanitation projects financed by the Bank throughout Asia, Africa, and Latin America. Participation can increase project success by incorporating user preferences and providing users with a sense of ownership of systems; but there needs to be better assessment or weighing of gender-specific costs of participatory approaches involving volunteer labor, especially for poor women.

The third dimension to increase infrastructure's benefits to women is including a user perspective in project design and implementation. Water supply and sanitation projects, in particular, demonstrate gender differences in preferences regarding systems design and the importance of considering women's preferences. In a Bank-funded water supply and sanitation project in Sri Lanka ($32.3 million with IDA credit of $24.3 million), it was observed that women and men in the community meetings disagreed as to whether to use tube wells, hand pump wells, or spring source gravity schemes and as to where to locate water sources. Women's preferences prevailed in this case because they were the primary users of the systems.

To include women's perspectives, infrastructure projects need to acknowledge women's productive as well as reproductive responsibilities and work to overcome constraints that may prevent women from participating or voicing their preferences in community institutions. A World Bank $28.3 million loan to upgrade homes and improve water and waste systems in urban slum and rural settlement areas in the Northwest Frontier Province in Pakistan has encountered the problem of women not participating in community meetings because of religious and cultural norms. To gain women's input for project planning, Bank staff initiated a pilot project in which a female staff member conducts meetings and interviews with female community members about their views regarding home upgrading and water systems. This pilot will be tested and used in the project if it is found to be effective in gaining women's input.

. . . .

EMPLOYMENT GENERATION FOR POOR WOMEN

■   SINCE THE MID-1970S GOVERNMENTS have used compensatory strategies to transfer income to and protect the poor from the effects of economic downturns and the short-term costs of structural adjustment policies and market oriented reforms. These instruments have generated short-term employment for the poor, and sometimes they have done so for poor women. But the literature that has analyzed these schemes' effectiveness in targeting the poor has for the most part underplayed gender-specific effects.[62] The employment effects on women of two kinds of programs discussed below offer suggestions to better target poor women with employment opportunities in World Bank compensatory lending.

PUBLIC WORKS AND SOCIAL FUNDS

The two types of compensatory strategies are centrally implemented public works employment schemes and social investment funds. The World Bank, in partnership with international and bilateral donors, has helped to design and underwrite the social funds. They include the Bolivian Social Emergency Fund (FSE) and the follow-up Social Investment Fund (FIS), and similar funds in many Latin American and Caribbean countries and in Africa.[63] Public works employment programs have instead relied mostly on domestic funding, through direct taxation or special government budget allocations. The best known, and the oldest public works program, is the Maharashtra Employment Guarantee Scheme (EGS) in India; others include emergency employment programs in Chile (the PEM and the POJH) and in Peru (PAIT) in the seventies and early eighties.[64]

Public works programs are top-down interventions by the state while social funds are designed to foster participation by NGOs, private sector firms, and communities in implementation. In this latter case the state funds but does not implement projects. Perhaps counterintuitively, the record of the supply-oriented government schemes in terms of reaching poor women and providing them with paid work is far better than that of the demand driven social funds. For instance, while FSE and the FIS generated *no* paid employment for women, about 43 percent of all the labor employed in EGS during the 1978–1988 decade was female.[65] This figure increased to 80 percent of the 374,000 workers employed by the PAIT in Peru, and to 52 percent of the workers at the height of the PEM in Chile (in 1982), when it was employing an average of 389,000 workers per month.[66]

FEATURES OF SUCCESS

Women's high participation rates in public works and emergency employment programs is associated, not with these programs' explicit intention to benefit women with work, but rather with their low wage rates and low skill requirements. In contrast, social funds have generally failed in providing employment to women (when employment creation is included in the funds) and in otherwise involving women and women's groups as main actors, that is, as fund solicitors and project implementors. This is not to say that women do not benefit from the social infrastructure built or the health care provided by social funds, but calls into question the notion that demand driven participatory strategies are in and of themselves sufficient to reach and benefit women. The success of social funds in reaching excluded or marginal groups, including women, is largely dependent on the focus and orientation of the intermediaries that implement the state-funded projects. The more successful or well-established NGOs, who are better qualified to win state bids and access the funds, usually do not represent women's interests well, while community organizations can be very hierarchical in nature and often do not include women.

The government-implemented public works programs collected statistics disaggregated by gender that were critical to knowing their coverage of women and to monitoring progress, and these programs' centralized nature clearly aided in data collection. The decentralized, multiple agency social funds have a much tougher time collecting comparable statistics, and this lack of information can hide both benefits to women and problems regarding women's participation. For instance, some reports suggest that women and children worked in FSE construction projects (as paid and unpaid workers) but there is no good documentation of this fact.[67]

The public works programs are an example, although perhaps an unintentional one, of government intervention to expand women's income generation opportunities and suggest the potential reach of well-designed public sector interventions that target women.

The EGS in India and the PAIT in Peru did not require prior training from workers, allowed flexible hours, recruited workers from nearby neighborhoods so that there were no transportation costs, and allowed women to bring their children to work. In addition, the PAIT had the objective of including 30 percent women among the workers. These shared features suggest design changes that can encourage women's participation in government employment programs without using price signals (lower wages) to imperfectly target women and compound existing market imperfections. Employment programs could increase women's participation without reinforcing wage discrimination by sex by providing a sufficiently varied range of employment options and executing agencies so as to include women but not completely feminize the program; utilizing women-based intermediaries and work options that include piece rate home-based production; providing work close to the home, setting flexible hours, and including options for childcare; defining an explicit policy to reach women and gather statistics disaggregated by sex; and avoiding setting different wage structures for men and women.

There are indications that the new generation of social investment funds in Latin America and the Caribbean and Africa is paying some attention to gender issues. For instance, Ecuador's social investment fund (started in 1993 with a projected total budget of $120 million, of which $30 million was a World Bank loan) collects data disaggregated by gender, and

Cameroon's Social Dimension of Adjustment Program (1991) included a WID component that was, however, affected by general lack of funds and closed down in 1993.[68] Future World Bank cofinanced social investment funds could significantly increase benefits to poor women by combining the positive features of centralized, supply-driven interventions with those of decentralized, demand oriented ones. They could benefit from the public sector's comparative advantage in generating short-term employment quickly, in reaching the excluded, and in collecting statistics, as well as from using private sector capacity in implementation, which can increase participation and long-term sustainability, promote accountability, and contribute to the institutional growth of NGOs.

Part V
Concluding Observations

MAJOR FINDINGS

■ THIS REVIEW OF SPECIFIC PROJECTS that have aimed to benefit women in major sectors of World Bank project lending does not purport to be an exhaustive evaluation of the largest development bank's work in this area. Nonetheless, staff interviews and a review of Bank documents leads to the following general findings.

■ The World Bank's efforts on behalf of women in the social sectors are significant, but for the most part still fairly recent. Lessons learned from individual projects need to be more widely spread. The focus of the Bank's effort needs now to advance from projects to policy; and as a part of the increased investment in social services for both women and men, the quality of, as well as the access to, social services needs greater attention. This raises difficult operational challenges for the World Bank. Nonetheless, it is notable that the Bank has taken a leadership role in these areas that offer significant benefits for women.

■ The same robust attention to particular impediments to increasing women's economic opportunities and earnings has yet to be made. Narrowly defined efforts—especially in agricultural extension—have been under way for years. But much more could be done to improve the contributions these services make to women; and greater efforts are needed in other areas, ranging from promoting reforms in property laws and banking regulation to increasing investments in rural roads and attacking biases against women in the formal labor market.

■ Across sectors, increasing the Bank's promotion of labor intensive growth and investments in poverty reduction policies and projects should result in increasing benefits to women who constitute some 70 percent of the world's absolute poor—as long as these investments provide employment opportunities for women and respond to the specific nature of women's poverty.

■ Under the circumstances of still limited know-how in specific areas, spotty institutional commitment to overcoming barriers to women, and inadequate core funding, it is too soon to rely fully on the mainstreaming of gender issues into operations. The World Bank's call to mainstream gender is a right long-term goal, but there is not enough operational expertise or a sufficient critical mass of convinced and trained staff to take for granted the successful impact on women of this approach in all areas of World Bank activity. Special emphasis on women and up-front investments are still required to build an adequate portfolio of Bank lending beneficial to women.

The experience of CIDA, an agency widely credited with leadership in the WID field, is illuminating in terms of mainstreaming. After an initial significant push on WID, senior management, increasingly consumed with other cross-cutting issues such as human rights and the environment, assumed (prematurely) that WID was "done"—that it had been mainstreamed into the agency's regular operations and therefore there was no longer a need for the strategic, catalytic role of CIDA's WID directorate. The WID unit was accordingly downsized and WID resources were significantly reduced. But a recent evaluation found that because the necessary commitment, skills, and resources were far from internalized throughout the institution, serious momentum had been lost with the declining emphasis on WID. In the mid-1990s, a new president, recognizing the need to rejuvenate CIDA's WID effort, reaffirmed WID as a priority, elevated the unit, and publicly rewarded several members of CIDA's staff for their work on behalf of women. The World Bank's new president should consider doing likewise.

This is where we saw the World Bank in the summer of 1995, on the eve of the Beijing Conference that year. With heightened international interest and new leadership, the Bank may well be poised to enter a new era on women's concerns. To more completely fulfill its mission of improving the lives of poor women, the World Bank will have to grapple with tough outstanding questions on best strategies and practices and create an enabling environment in which staff is equipped and encouraged to treat this as a priority concern.

. . . .

DEFINING BEST PRACTICES

■   UNRESOLVED BEST PRACTICES QUESTIONS include targeting versus universal interventions, minimalist versus multiple actions, projects versus policy, and support of NGOs versus government.

Targeting the poor is commonplace to reduce costs and increase benefits to them. But targeting has administrative as well as political costs, and benefits can leak to the nonpoor.[69] The costs of targeting the poor apply equally well in the case of interventions targeted to women, and these costs may be the source of some of the institutional resistance to stand-alone women's projects. Self-targeting (where projects' benefits or resources are in theory available to all, but in practice only of interest to the poor) is a more attractive alternative that minimizes political and administrative costs. Maternal and child health as well as nutrition interventions and family planning programs have traditionally self-targeted women successfully. In addition, microfinance projects, because of the way loans are structured, and public works programs, largely because of the below market wages they offer, have become good examples of self-targeting and have succeeded in increasing women's access to financial services and to (low-paid) public employment without the need to exclude men from applying for project benefits.

Nonetheless, targeting women was needed and worked well in many other interventions we reviewed, including, for instance, targeting girls with scholarships in situations where there was a wide gender gap in schooling and targeting women farmers with agricultural extension services. The more project benefits are attractive to and can be appropriated by men, the higher the need to target women in project implementation, but also the higher the potential costs of targeting. This is a tradeoff that project implementors need to anticipate and guard against or minimize, especially in the productive sectors, where project benefits (such as new technologies, loans, and access to other productive resources) are equally attractive to both men and women.

MINIMALISM

Projects that, for instance, give women access to credit and reform financial markets will not perform well or be sustainable over the long term without parallel interventions. Such measures are of the sort that insure women's access to technical training and modern technology, or that improve rural roads, or that permit women to own assets. Projects that increase women's access to wage employment work best when complementary interventions provide childcare options and access to health services. Even more common are health and family planning interventions that give rise to the need for parallel action to increase women's income.

The awareness that a package of cross-sectoral interventions is required has often clashed with the realities of women's lives and the restricted implementation capacity in developing countries. This has resulted in project failures when a single project, as is the case of some Bank project loans in different sectors, undertakes too many different, often specialized, and sometimes incompatible tasks, as noted in the earlier discussion on credit. The temptation to undertake multiple action is commonplace given women's interrelated productive and reproductive roles and the many obstacles they face, but needs to be tempered by better understanding of women's time burdens and technical and institutional constraints. Simple interventions are usually more easy to implement well and contribute to explaining the success of education projects, agricultural extension efforts, and minimalist credit interventions for women. However, simple interventions need to be set in an effective overall policy framework for them to be able to reap longer-term and more sustainable benefits.

POLICY REFORM

Although projects that benefit women are needed, they are insufficient without broad economy-wide and sectoral policy changes. Changes might include depreciation of overvalued exchange rates, liberalization of agricultural producer prices, removal of restrictions on the movement and marketing of agricultural inputs and products. Agricultural extension targeted to women farmers without agricultural policies that encourage smallholder agriculture and off-farm employment will not work to raise rural women's incomes. Neither increased extension services for women nor education reforms will benefit women as intended without accompanying labor-intensive infrastructural policy reform and development. Nor will it work to expand women's access to credit and savings without broad financial sector reforms and interventions that lead to the efficient functioning of private financial institutions. More generally, World Bank policy and project lending is required to raise the productivity of small farmers and entrepreneurs as well as low-income people's access to basic health, education, and jobs. Such generalized lending is needed to benefit the majority of women who are poor and over-represented among low-wage workers, small producers, and small entrepreneurs. The Bank can play a major role in shaping these necessary actions.

PUBLIC-SECTOR ROLE

Historically, NGOs—many of them women-based—have taken the lead in promoting action that benefits women in developing countries. It is therefore not surprising that the Bank, whose main client is governments, has followed rather than led in the WID area. It is also not surprising that much of the World Bank lending that is directed to women includes NGOs in advocacy or implementation. Women-based NGOs, by their very nature, have a far easier time reaching women clients than other organizations in either the public or private sector. Because they work on a smaller scale, they can also more easily experiment with alternative interventions. But there are tradeoffs involved when working through these organizations. The review of projects in education that in the past have relied substantially on NGOs for implementation reveals the need to scale up interventions. There is a need to foster changes in national programs and policies that will enable implementing on a larger scale the changes brought about by NGOs.

Even as countries move to reform, and in many cases downsize the roles that their governments play in their economies, it remains clear that the public sector has a crucial role to play in increasing women's opportunities and well-being. It is also clear that the public sector's role in this area needs to be expanded, against the tide. The Bank is uniquely positioned to influence national policies towards women in its dialogue with governments. The Bank could provide intellectual and financial leadership to governments. If it sharpens and strengthens its research and analysis, it can also provide governments with best practices know-how and services. Such support to governments is both necessary and compatible with expansion of the definition of the Bank's clientele to include civil society—twin elements of a major role for the Bank in improving women's conditions.

. . . .

CREATING ENABLING CONDITIONS WITHIN THE WORLD BANK

■ A NECESSARY UNDERPINNING of the World Bank's efforts in the different sectors is a set of central, crosscutting enabling conditions. In order to realize the Bank's full potential to increase women's well-being, Bank staff must be committed to the overall goal of benefiting women and have the capacity needed to address women's issues effectively. Staff commitment to any issue in the Bank is enhanced by a combination of: 1) evidence that the issue warrants attention and that it will be seen as convincing both within the Bank and in borrower countries; 2) clearly expressed senior management and board interest and support; and 3) resources to support efforts. Capacity can be developed through a combination of staff diversification, technical assistance and training, dissemination of best practice, and the provision of adequate analytic, human and financial resources. Strengthening the enabling environment within the Bank by increasing investments in research and implementing management initiatives would seem particularly salient at the present time.

RESEARCH

It is demonstrably the case that the marshaling of solid evidence of the benefits to growth and economic efficiency of investing in women has been a powerful factor in raising the profile of the issue of women in development. Statistics on the unequal status of women have been available for years; but equity arguments alone were not enough to stimulate concerted action. The importance of continued, indeed expanded research cannot therefore be overstated, especially now on issues pertaining to the productive sectors, where knowledge and action lags as noted by the Bank itself, in its paper for Beijing. Salient is the need for empirical work on the extent, determinants, and consequences of women's productivity and income in agriculture as well as in informal and formal labor markets. This should also include reliable data on the reasonable assumption that poverty is becoming feminized.

Although much of the earliest work on women in development came from outside, the World Bank has made important contributions both through its own documents and through research it has commissioned on such issues as women's education (including studies of the determinants of female education in each of five regions), women and fertility, women's health, and to a lesser extent women in the labor force. But there is a great deal more research and policy analysis that is needed on the gender dimensions of development at both the micro- and macro-economic levels, as well as in the linkages between the two.

An important component of this role is undertaking empirical research on these linkages to achieve better understanding of the impact of macroeconomic reforms on women and of the way these reforms need to be restructured to benefit them. The continuing debate on the impact of structural adjustment programs on the situation of women in developing countries could use systematic research of this kind.[70] Research that measures women's work and economic contributions and that links changes in macroeconomic variables with changes in the situation of particular subpopulations is challenging and costly. The Bank is one of the few institutions that has the resources to do this research.

The World Bank has the potential, should it choose to use it, to be a leader in the domain of research on women's productivity, income, and poverty.

MANAGEMENT

There was a perception among some within the Bank prior to James Wolfensohn's arrival to the presidency of the the Bank, that management support for WID/gender was waning. Probably nothing could be more important at the beginning of a new president's term than for top management to send a loud and clear signal that this is not the case. Mr. Wolfensohn's speech in Beijing did this, as did the series of follow-up activities aimed at building momentum for continued attention to the conference's agenda for action. Simple pronouncements of concern on the occasion of a special conference on women are not sufficient, however, especially in an institution where many of whose staff remain skeptical that there is as yet substantial evidence of economic returns from investing in women. What is needed, as has occurred in the case of education, is sustained commitment of adequate resources (staff *and* money), if the signal is to be viewed as more than mere lip service.

Within the Bank there is now a central unit responsible for WID/gender analysis and operational support. It has an important role to play in conveying that this issue is an institutional priority. This unit was probably most influential between 1986 and 1991, when it benefited from visible support from then-president Barber Conable. For most of that time (1987–1993) the unit was a separate division within the Population and Human Resources Department (PHRWD). The present incarnation of this unit, the Gender Analysis and Policy group, is a thematic area of the Poverty and Social Policy Department within the Human Capital Development and Operations Policy Vice Presidency. Although embedding the unit this way may be consistent with the Bank's institutional mainstreaming of WID, its lower profile is sending the wrong message at a time when there is, unfortunately, still a need for advocacy in certain quarters.

At best, however, the central gender analysis unit can only be an expert voice and catalyst. If the goal of improving the status of women is to be firmly embedded in the activities of the Bank, operational staff will have to have the incentive as well as knowledge and skills to translate that policy into action. Those directly responsible for implementing the Bank's gender policies observe that their very limited resources make monitoring staff to ensure they address gender issues unrealistic. Furthermore, most feel that, given the often skeptical climate in which they work, a collegial approach to encouraging attention to women is likely to yield the best results. Under present circumstances, the top layers of management, supported by the board, have primary responsibility for creating the climate in which that approach will flourish. Modest help might be provided by citations, awards, or other forms of acknowledgment of impressive staff efforts. But in the final analysis, it is where the leadership must devote staff, research, and financial resources to make the difference.

SPECIAL FUNDS/RESOURCES

One useful tool has been the availability of extrabudgetary resources to do what the Bank considers innovative work, meaning activities such as participation and gender/social analysis that are not established practice, or operations research that is more tentative and exploratory than the typical best-practices analysis.

Many task managers have accessed additional resources for such work through various trust fund arrangements with bilateral donors, particularly Canada, Japan, the Netherlands, and the Nordic countries. A common use of these concessional monies is the hiring of consultants with specific expertise to assist in project design, implementation, and monitoring. The exact extent to which these funds are used to support gender-specific work is not clear because the Bank categorizes allocations only by sector and not activity. But anecdotal evidence suggests that a considerable amount of the Bank's gender work is supported by external money in some way. And those who would commend the Bank for what it executes in the area of WID/gender should recognize that a good portion of that effort has been stimulated by grant money from other donors.

In many ways, access to trust funds has often served as an avenue for staff to overcome internal budget limitations or the low priority accorded this work. Because a staff member could apply for and secure funding from a donor directly, Bank management could hardly object to a proposed activity on budgetary grounds. Similarly, the system has also provided outside donors with an opportunity to leverage attention to particular issues through their provision of earmarked concessional resources.

These circumstances can give rise to a perception that "freelancing" individuals and outside donors may be driving Bank lending; they generate administrative costs and complications associated with managing external resources under multiple contract. For these reasons, the Bank has begun to reform procedures to create a more centralized, streamlined system whereby management is better able to ensure that the uses of outside money reflect predetermined Bank priorities.

The goals of the restructuring are not only sensible from an institutional standpoint, they are also consistent with the objective of institutionally mainstreaming gender. If those who choose to focus on gender issues can reliably access external money to do it, what incentive is there for the Bank to internalize these activities and make them part of regular budget allocations? But there are risks entailed in centralization: If much of the Bank's push on women's issues is going to have to depend on individual initiative, as it presently does, this funding stream may be a necessary evil. Furthermore, even if staff commitment were universal, the capacity within the Bank to do this work is quite uneven, suggesting that there is still a need for supplemental resources.

WOMEN IN THE BANK

It would be incorrect to say that attention to the issue of how women's lives are being affected by development has been advanced only by women within the World Bank. Nevertheless, women on staff, in positions of management, and on the board have been instrumental in building the case for recognizing the role of women in development on efficiency as well as equity grounds. They have helped to design experimental projects that demonstrate how to overcome past neglect, and to push the bureaucracy to pay attention to the findings and results. Indeed, behind the important 1992 speech by Lawrence Summers on girls' education and Barber Conable's priority on investing in women's health (Safe Motherhood Initiative of 1987), lie years of independent and collaborative work on the part of advocates inside and outside the Bank, the vast majority of them women. This is not to imply that only women worry about women; but it is widely said within the World Bank itself that the role of women on staff, in management, and on the board has been crucially important.

At the same time, it must be noted that, especially in recent years, many men in the Bank have taken an active research or operational role in the issue of women's participation in and benefits from development; in some cases, they have been more effective in their advocacy of gender issues than women. Indeed, according to some staff, male attention to WID/gender in what is still a predominantly male institution often helps legitimize and professionalize the issue. However, both men and women underscore the lack of status afforded this work within the Bank and many, especially women, feel that association with gender expertise can be a serious liability for their careers.

Obviously, therefore, the way to broaden and deepen attention to women in World Bank activities ought to include, but not be limited to, hiring more women staff, especially at management and senior management levels. According to its own calculations, although women account for 51 percent of the Bank's staff and 30 percent of professional staff, they form only 12 percent of managers and 8 percent of senior managers.[71] It is notable, therefore, that Mr. Wolfensohn's first three management appointments, made within his first four months in office, happened to be women: Vice President for Finance and Planning, International Finance Corporation (IFC); General Counsel, IFC; and creation of a Chief of Staff role at the vice president level. In addition, he has appointed the first-ever female managing director. But that has to be seen as only a start. Moreover, given the role that the board of directors and member governments play in shaping Bank policy and action, it is notable that until 1994, there had been a total of only two women directors in the history of the Bank; and there are now only three women out of 24 directors.[72] It is also interesting to note that the proportion of women staff is lowest in those areas that this report highlighted as having "unrealized opportunities." Increasing female staff offers no guarantee that needed research and operational activities will take place, especially in the current climate where women feel that focusing on gender issues may somehow jeopardize their careers. What the Bank can and should do is to remove the stigma associated with gender work by reorienting institutional priorities and actively reinforcing staff efforts to address the role of women in development.

Mr. Wolfensohn's speech at the 1995 Beijing Conference and his immediate appointment of women to senior management positions bodes well in terms of fostering a more receptive environment for increased efforts that will benefit women. In addition, however, Mr. Wolfensohn needs to follow the commitments he made at Beijing with a clear and broad-ranging institutional strategy, backed by staff and resources, to devote the institution's research, advisory, and financial resources to the goal of investing in women and to work in conjunction with other institutions whose mandates and instrumentalities support efforts that complement that which the World Bank is well equipped to do.

Notes

[1] Josette Murphy, *Gender Issues in Bank Lending* (Washington, DC: World Bank, 1995).

[2] The selection criteria were project documents that contained specific actions directed to women at the appraisal stage, and the analysis is therefore about *intended* rather than *implemented* actions.

[3] Ruth Leger Sivard, *Women . . . A World Survey*, 2nd edition (Washington, DC: World Priorities, 1995); Barbara Herz and Anthony R. Measham, "The Safe Motherhood Initiative: Proposals for Action," World Bank Discussion Paper No. 9 (Washington, DC: World Bank, 1987).

[4] International Center for Research on Women (ICRW), "Where Women Stand: Gains and Gaps in Women's Lives," ICRW Global Fact Sheet (Washington, DC: ICRW, 1995).

[5] Mayra Buvinić, Rekha Mehra, and Annelies Drost-Maasry, "Gender in Perspective: Trends in Social and Economic Indicators," report prepared for the UNDP's *1995 Human Development Report* (Washington, DC: ICRW, 1994).

[6] United Nations Development Programme, *Human Development Report 1995* (New York: Oxford University Press, 1995); Idriss Jazairy, Mohiuddin Alamgir, and Theresa Panuccio, *The State of World Rural Poverty* (New York: New York University Press for IFAD, 1992).

[7] Sivard, op. cit.

[8] Sivard, op. cit.

[9] World Bank, *Advancing Gender Equality: From Concept to Action* (Washington, DC: World Bank, 1995).

[10] James D. Wolfensohn, "Women and the Transformation of the 21st Century," address to the Fourth U.N. World Conference on Women, Beijing, September 15, 1995.

[11] It could be argued, however, that this conclusion ignores the powerful influence of the Bank's policy lending, which may have a larger impact on women's productive activities than the project lending reviewed in this report. The evidence required to support this statement is not available (as there is no reliable database on these activities). However, there are indications that the beneficial effects of economic policy lending on productivity are often not gender neutral, but favor men over women. For instance, it is believed that the decontrol of domestic producer prices in Nigeria after 1986 benefited men more than women because it boosted production of cash crops (cocoa and rubber in control of men with adequate landholdings and access to credit to grow such crops). Without access to these resources, women subsistence farmers (growing, among others, cassava in the south and millet in the north) were unable to both move into commercial production and reap the benefits of the domestic output increases resulting from policy reform.

[12] See section in this essay on "Women's Status Worldwide"; and UNDP, op. cit.

[13] Barber Conable, "The Safe Motherhood Initiative," Address and Proposals for Action, Nairobi, Kenya, February 10, 1995; and Lawrence H. Summers, "Investing in All the

People: Educating Women in Developing Countries," prepared for a Development Economics Seminar at the 1992 World Bank Annual Meetings (Washington, DC: World Bank, 1992).

[14] Murphy, op. cit.

[15] World Bank, *Enhancing Women's Participation in Economic Development*, World Bank Policy Paper (Washington, DC: World Bank, 1994); and World Bank, *Toward Gender Equality: The Role of Public Policy* (Washington, DC: World Bank, 1995).

[16] Kevin M. Cleaver and Gotz A. Schreiber, *Reversing the Spiral: The Population, Agriculture, and Environment Nexus in Sub-Saharan Africa* (Washington, DC: World Bank, 1994); and George Psacharopoulos and Zafiris Tzannatos, *Women's Employment and Pay in Latin America: Overview and Methodology*, World Bank Regional and Sectoral Studies (Washington, DC: World Bank, 1992).

[17] Ester Boserup, *Woman's Role in Economic Development* (New York: St. Martin's Press, 1970).

[18] World Bank, *Toward Gender Equality*, op. cit.

[19] In light of this fact, the evaluation recommends that in the future CIDA place a greater emphasis on targeted interventions for women. See CIDA, "Gender as a Cross-Cutting Theme in Development Assistance: An Evaluation of CIDA's WID Policy and Activities, 1984–1992" (Ottawa: CIDA, 1993).

[20] Shahra Razavi and Carol Miller, "Gender Mainstreaming: A Study of Efforts by the UNDP, the World Bank, and the ILO to Institutionalize Gender Issues," UNRISD Occasional Paper No. 4 (Geneva: UNRISD, 1995), p. viii.

[21] World Bank, *Enhancing Women's Participation*, op. cit.; and World Bank, *Toward Gender Equality*, op. cit.

[22] Margaret Goodman, "Ex-Post Evaluation on Social Investment Fund: El Salvador Loan 861/SF-ES" (Washington, DC: Inter-American Development Bank, 1995).

[23] The global burden of disease (GBD) is a measure of the impact of 100 diseases and injuries in terms of premature death and disability. For details on the method of calculation and the assumptions upon which GBD is based, see World Bank, *World Bank Development Report 1993* (New York: Oxford University Press, 1993).

[24] World Bank, *World Development Report 1993*, op. cit.

[25] World Bank, *A New Agenda for Women's Health and Nutrition* (Washington, DC: World Bank, 1994).

[26] World Bank, *World Development Report 1993*, op. cit.

[27] Proponents of expanding the initiative (including many in the Bank) argued that a limited focus on one interval in a woman's life (motherhood) misses the full range of women's health issues and that a focus on *mortality* obscures the extent of reproductive health issues that cause considerable suffering but do not result in death. Others suggested that broadening the scope might weaken support for the initiative and that a narrow focus was more pragmatic both politically and operationally. The resolution to this debate may have been hastened in part by the onslaught of AIDS, which has forced attention to reproductive health issues beyond "safe motherhood," i.e., sexually transmitted diseases.

[28] J. Joseph Speidel, "Population Policy for the 21st Century: Setting Priorities, Paying for Programs," presented at the Third Session of the Preparatory Committee for the ICPD, United Nations, New York, April 4, 1994.

[29] "Gender," however, still refers primarily to women—with the exception of a few responsible parenthood messages, the role of men in population programs is still largely neglected.

[30] Susan Hill Cochrane, "Fertility and Education: What Do We Really Know?" World Bank Staff Occasional Papers, No. 26 (Baltimore, MD: Johns Hopkins University Press, 1979).

[31] Conable, op. cit.

[32] Lawrence H. Summers, "Investing in All the People," Policy Research Working Paper Series, No. 905 (Washington, DC: World Bank, May 1992).

[33] Wolfensohn, op. cit.

[34] Herz and Measham, op. cit.

[35] Robert Picciotto and Rachel Weaving, "A New Project Cycle for the World Bank?" *Finance and Development*, Vol. 31, No. 4 (December 1994), pp. 42–44.

[36] Elizabeth M. King and M. Anne Hill, eds., *Women's Education in Developing Countries: Barriers, Benefits, and Policy* (Baltimore, MD: Johns Hopkins University Press, 1993), p. 260.

[37] World Bank, *Enhancing Women's Participation*, op. cit.

[38] Harold Alderman, personal communication, June 1995.

[39] King and Hill, op. cit.

[40] For example, it has been found in Brazil that improving the quality of primary education may require additional expenditure immediately, but will eventually *reduce* costs per pupil because it will lower dropout and repeater rates. R.F. Harbison and E.A. Hanusek, *Educational Performance of the Poor: Lessons from Rural Northeast Brazil* (New York: Oxford University Press, 1992).

[41] Although the World Bank has only in recent years expanded contacts with NGOs and has just opened a loan window to lend directly to NGOs in microfinance, the IDB has had this capacity for over 15 years through a small projects credit line. The IDB's longer history of interaction with NGOs can help to expalin their better WID/gender record in Latin America and the Caribbean.

[42] As of June 1995, the highest representation of women in World Bank group staff by sector, excluding administrative categories, was in social sciences (53 percent) and personnel/human resources (42 percent). The lowest representation was in industry and energy (14 percent), agriculture (14 percent), and public sector management (28 percent). Information provided by the Management and Personnel Services Department, World Bank.

[43] C. Mark Blackden and Elizabeth Morris-Hughes, "Paradigm Postponed: Gender and Economic Adjustment in Sub-Saharan Africa," Technical Department, Africa Region, Technical Note No. 13 (Washington, DC: World Bank, 1993).

[44] Robert Paarlberg, *Countrysides at Risk: The Political Geography of Sustainable Agriculture*, Policy Essay No. 16 (Washington, DC: Overseas Development Council, 1994).

[45] Many internal Bank WID reviews find impressively high percentages of Bank project documents with attention to women. For example, one report notes that in 1992, 88 percent of all agriculture projects in East Asia, 67 percent in South Asia, and 60 percent in Africa

incorporated gender analysis and/or proposed specific activities to benefit women. However, these same reviews note that such measurements are often meaningless because of differences of subjectivity in standards and because of the frequent discrepancies between project intent and outcomes.

[46] Agnes R. Quisumbing et al., "Women: The Key to Food Security" (Washington, DC: International Food Policy Research Institute, 1995).

[47] World Bank, "A Review of Bank Lending for Agricultural Credit and Rural Finance," Operations Evaluation Report No. 12143 (Washington, DC: World Bank, 1993).

[48] Jacob Yaron, "Successful Rural Finance Institutions," World Bank Discussion Paper No. 150 (Washington, DC: World Bank, 1992); and World Bank, "A Review of Bank Lending for Agricultural Credit," op. cit.

[49] Judith Tendler, "Whatever Happened to Poverty Alleviation?" *World Development*, Vol. 17, No. 7 (1989); and Tyler S. Biggs, Donald Snodgrass, and Pradeep Saivastava, "On Minimalist Credit Programs, " Development Discussion Paper No. 331 (Cambridge, MA: Harvard Institute for International Development, 1990).

[50] Elisabeth Rhyne and Sharon Holt, "Women in Finance and Enterprise Development," Education and Social Policy Department Discussion Paper No. 40 (Washington, DC: World Bank, 1994).

[51] Leila M. Webster, Randall Riopelle, and Anne-Marie Chidzero, "World Bank Lending for Small Enterprises 1989–1993," draft report (Washington, DC: World Bank, 1994).

[52] Mayra Buvinić, "Projects for Women in the Third World: Explaining Their Misbehavior," *World Development*, Vol. 24, No. 5 (1986), pp. 653–64.

[53] Rhyne and Holt, op. cit.

[54] Yaron, op. cit.

[55] Marguerite Berger and Mayra Buvinić, eds., *Women's Ventures: Assistance to the Informal Sector in Latin America* (West Hartford, CT: Kumarian Press, 1989); and Maria Margarita Guzmán and María Clemencia Castro, "From a Woman's Guarantee Fund to a Bank for Microenterprise: Process and Results," in Berger and Buvinić, op. cit.

[56] "The Missing Links: Financial Systems That Work for the Majority," Report of the Women's World Banking Global Policy Forum, April 1995.

[57] Boserup, op. cit.; and Irene Tinker, "The Adverse Impact of Development on Women," in *Women and World Development*, ed. Irene Tinker, Michèle Bo Bramsen, and Mayra Buvinić (New York: Praeger, 1976).

[58] Erica Royston and Sue Armstrong, eds., *Preventing Maternal Deaths* (Geneva: World Health Organization, 1989).

[59] T. Castañeda, "Los Determinantes del Descenso de la Mortalidad Infantil en Chile, 1975–82," *Cuadernos de Economía* (Santiago: Universidad de Chile, 1985).

[60] Guy Standing, "Global Feminization Through Flexible Labor," *World Development*, Vol. 17, No. 7 (1989), pp. 1077–95.

[61] World Bank, *Enhancing Women's Participation*, op. cit.

[62] Carol Graham, *Safety Nets, Politics, and the Poor: Transitions to Market Economies* (Washington, DC: The Brookings Institution, 1994); Martin Ravallion, "Reaching the Rural

Poor Through Public Employment," *World Bank Research Observer*, Vol. 6, No. 2 (1991), pp. 153–75; and PREALC/OIT, *Empleos de Emergencia* (Santiago: Organización Internacional de Trabajo, 1988).

[63] The FSE mobilized total funds of $198.1 million. The World Bank contributed with IDA credits that added $26.8 million. The FIS has expected lifetime investments of $140 million, with IDA credits of approximately $62 million.

[64] The EGS began in 1975 with a budget of $22.3 million rupees. In 1984–85, it spent about 2,000 million rupees to create about 178 million person-days employment. Between October 1985 and June 1987, the PAIT in Peru provided temporary work to about 374,000 workers with an investment of $100 million. In 1987, the PEM in Chile employed an average of 40,600 workers per month with a cost of roughly $350,000. In the same year, the POJH employed 75,700 monthly workers at a cost of $1.4 million.

[65] Sarthi Acharya and V.G. Panwalker, *The Maharashtra Employment Guarantee Scheme: Impacts on Male and Female Labor* (Bangkok: The Population Council, Regional Office for South and East Asia, 1988).

[66] Maria Elena Vigier, "La Participación de las Mujeres en el PAIT," mimeo, 1987.

[67] Molly Pollack, "Feminization of the Informal Sector in Latin America and the Caribbean," Serie Mujer y Desarrollo No. 11, LC/L.731 (Santiago: Economic Commission for Latin America and the Caribbean, 1993).

[68] The revised total costs of the Cameroon Social Dimension of Adjustment Program were $49 million, with a World Bank IDA contribution of $21.5 million.

[69] Amartya Sen, "The Political Economy of Targeting," in *Public Spending and the Poor: Theory and Evidence*, ed. Dominique van de Walle and Kimberly Nead (Baltimore, MD: Johns Hopkins University Press, 1995).

[70] The need for this research is underscored by the Bank's own reports, including one written in 1993 and another in 1995. The 1993 report, which explored gender dimensions of adjustment in Sub-Saharan Africa, found that improvements would require the following: 1) more understanding of the labor implications of adjustment measures on women; 2) more gender analysis in the design of policies and programs that take account of such things as the gender division of labor, diversity of household and intrahousehold relationships, and control over economically productive resources; and 3) more research and analysis of the different time constraints affecting men and women. (See Blackden and Morris-Hughes, op. cit.)

While the capacity of people to respond to economic opportunities is significantly influenced by gender-based factors, insufficient understanding of the causes of poverty, including its gender dimensions, and how they might be remedied remains a fundamental stumbling block to the design and monitoring of poverty-reduction efforts. See Report of an African Region Task Force, "Taking Action for Poverty Reduction in Sub-Saharan Africa" (Washington, DC: World Bank, August 31, 1995), draft; and see also Nilüfer Çağatay, Diane Elson, and Caren Grown, eds., *Gender, Adjustment and Economics, World Development*, Special Issue, Vol. 23, No. 11 (November 1995).

[71]Martha M. Hamilton, "World Bank Urges Nations to Invest More in Women," *The Washington Post*, August 25, 1995, p. 26.

[72]It should be further noted that there were no women on the 18-member Development Committee Task Force charged with proposing long-term reforms of the World Bank and other MDBs, and regularly there are no women government representatives at the meetings of the Development Committee, which Mr. Wolfensohn has said he wants to see play more of an engaged policy role.

Appendix:
Excerpted Remarks from
ODC/ICRW Conference

The Role of MDBs in Improving the Status of Women

On July 21, 1995 the International Center for Research on Women and the Overseas Development Council brought together experts from the multilateral development banks, the United Nations, and other organizations to discuss the evolving status of women and the role of multilateral institutions in supporting their continued progress. Following are excerpted remarks delivered at the conference by Nancy Birdsall, Executive Vice President of the Inter-American Development Bank; Mahbub ul Haq, then Special Advisor to the Administrator of the U. N. Development Programme; Margaret Catley-Carlson, President of The Population Council; and Sven Sandström, Managing Director of the World Bank.

. . . .

THE EVOLVING STATUS OF WOMEN: IN THE ECONOMY, IN SOCIETY, AND IN DEVELOPMENT THINKING

NANCY BIRDSALL

I would like to convey two messages. The first has to do with the topic of this session: the *evolution* in thinking on women in development. It is that *evolution* may not be the right word. Progress has occurred, but it certainly has not been orderly, which might be thought with the term evolution. It has been stop and go.

The second message is that because we in the multilateral development banks (MDBs) reflect our shareholders' views, we are not likely to be at the academic frontier, not likely to be leaders in major new thinking on specific issues. But, on the other hand, because we are big and influential, we can be critical in shaping the way new thinking is developed and what happens. We can and should be leaders among the followers.

Regarding my first message, on the disorderly progress of thinking on women in development (WID), let me give you my impressions as a development economist. I find it helpful to think about how development economics as a field has evolved over the last two or three decades, and then consider how that has affected our thinking about the role of women in the development process.

We could crudely characterize the first several decades after the end of World War II as the "planning period"—a period when there was a view that governments, including those in developing countries, could manage the growth process—that policy could be right and programs would be done well. During this planning period, and particularly in the 1960s and 1970s, there was a focus on new thinking at the sectoral level about what could be done. I began my own career as a development economist with work on population in the 1970s. In the field of population, women emerged initially as the object of family planning programs. There was a lot of discussion about the status of women and fertility and about the notion that if women could be put to work, particularly in modern-sector jobs, then they would apparently have fewer children. Thinking in this area has evolved tremendously between the early 1970s and the recent world conference in Cairo. The issue is characterized very differently today, with a more appropriate emphasis on women as decision makers and on the welfare of the family. And of course even in the early 1970s there were certainly people, and in particular women, concerned with not only the effect of the status of women on fertility but also the effect on women of having many children and having very little control over their reproductive lives.

In the sectors of education and health during this "planning period," women were seen as beneficiaries or as non-beneficiaries of education and health programs. Then, as work emerged on agriculture and what the government could do to improve productivity in agriculture, women came to be seen as workers, itself a step forward. In particular, Ester Boserup's work on women in agriculture in Africa was important.

This is a very crude characterization of a period of planning when the state was seen as a potential manager of the growth process.

Meanwhile, in the 1970s, the new home economics of the family was emerging. That work, led by Gary Becker, who some years later won the Nobel Prize, made students of development more conscious of the fact that development had to do with the use of people's time and not only with money, and with factors—such as fertility, productive activities in the home, production of health of children—which are the usual domain of women and which had not been considered in the traditional economic work on development. Work on women's use of time in the home showed that women were bearing a double burden. It led to the quantification of something we all knew: Women were working at home and were also working for remuneration. Whether paid or unpaid, they were in the work force. And later when concern emerged about the environment, women began to be seen even more as a part of a larger system—both as perpetrators of a problem associated with poverty and as saviors who nurtured mother earth and seemed to be more concerned with sustainability of systems than did men.

In the 1980s the emphasis shifted again—necessarily to structural adjustment and stabilization programs. The emphasis shifted to the problem of ensuring that government did not interfere so much in the market system that it created its own distortions. There was a sense that government needed to be gotten off the backs of people.

In this period, women were absent, which reflected in part the focus of getting government out of the system. Traditionally, efforts for women have been seen as something that needed to be planned and managed, in which the state as a benign actor had to take some role.

As the work on adjustment proceeded, more emphasis emerged on public financing issues, in particular on analysis of taxes and of public expenditure and of what groups were paying and benefiting from government income and government spending. From this emerged a renewed concern with poverty and, in particular, with safety nets. In this context, among people concerned with women in development, it became clear that poverty is a women's issue: Women are the face of the poor. Facts emerged about the extent to which women head households and female-headed households are much more likely to be poor, and about the economic vulnerability of women—so many of whom bear the double burden of home production and work for pay.

Now in the 1990s, still another phase is emerging, at least in Latin America. In Latin America, there has been a successful period of critical economic reforms: first, fiscal stabilization; second, freeing up of trade regimes, ensuring that the economies would be open to global competition; and third, privatization to lift from societies and governments the burden of inefficient state enterprises. Particularly in the last couple of years, increasing attention has gone to complementing these reforms with re-creation of an effective state. The effective state is not the state of the pre-1980s period that manages everything; rather it is a lean and clean state that does the right thing: an effective state that ensures that government delivers social programs, manages the pension system prudently, introduces appropriate regulation of the environment, and begins to work through and with institutions of civil society—nongovernmental organizations (NGOs).

In Latin America, in part through these institutions of civil society, there has been a tremendous increase in the participation of all members of society in the development process, in political processes, and in social programs. It is in this context that women have emerged in a more active role as participants, indeed, as leaders, of programs at the community level and increasingly as participants at the political level.

So, in this grand sweep of the last three and a half decades in development, we have seen women as objects of programs and then as beneficiaries or non-beneficiaries, women as workers and therefore as contributors, women as the face of the poor, and most recently women as participants and leaders.

Let me turn quickly now to my second message, regarding the role of the MDBs—my impressions as a development bureaucrat at the Inter-American Development Bank (IDB). I will only give you one important fact about the IDB: I see tremendous progress on the women in development issue. In the IDB, 71 percent of the projects in the environment sector, 47 percent of those in education and health, 40 percent of those in agriculture, and 25 percent of those in sanitation and urban development incorporate special consideration for women's needs and their potential contribution in their design. This is the outcome of work by the IDB's Women in Development unit, which sets a high standard for ensuring the incorporation of gender considerations in project designs. These numbers reflect more than discussion in a report about women; they reflect something real in those projects—real in their design and in their use of resources.

Why this progress in a development bureaucracy? There is an important reality about the IDB and the other MDBs: Management and staff respond to shareholders—both to non-borrowers and obviously to borrowers. When the borrowers are concerned about an issue, it should and does make a big difference as to what the MBDs do. What we see in Latin America is a growing movement of participation of women at the community level and increasingly at the political level; these women are beginning to create more and more demands in their own communities and on their own governments for attention to women's needs and women's potential contribution in development activities. A critical role for the IDB is to foster and respond to this kind of demand-creation among our borrowers. When the IDB and other MDBs support the institutions of civil society, for example, we are supporting the creation of stronger demands on us, through increasing participation, including of women.

So my impression as a development bureaucrat is that progress is possible and is happening on incorporation of women and gender issues in development programs—because our shareholders and in particular our borrowers want this progress. We must obviously build on and consolidate this progress.

Let me end with my impressions as a woman about lessons and next steps for the development community and therefore for the MDBs. First, more thinking is needed about how we can ensure that women benefit from structural reforms. Globalization of the economy and a level playing field have the potential to penalize those who do not come to the game with all the equipment they need. As we support these necessary reforms, we must also continue to support the need for affirmative action—to ensure women gain access to education, credit, land—all the equipment that allows them to enter the economic game on equal terms with men.

Second, we in the development field need to put men back into the family. I was impressed by the recent publication from The Population Council on the family and in particular on the issue of the need for men to be involved in family life—not only as breadwinners but as nurturers. Behind every liberated woman, you will probably find a liberated man—a man who has begun to take real responsibility in the family, particularly for the children. Female-headed households, where there is no nurturing father, are only the most extreme signs of a pathology that needs to be addressed. Women need to take the lead in urging men to enter fully into family life. And the MDBs need to think through in a program sense what it means to put men back into the family.

Finally, a retrograde thought: Women have to be involved as women in the MDBs and in the development business if we are going to continue to see the progress that we have seen so far. Women have been the leaders in putting women's issues on the development agenda. And though it is true that when women and men are both really liberated, women will no doubt act like men, and men (one hopes!) more like women, we cannot rest yet—not until the day when we who are women can afford to act like men and not worry about the special needs and the lost contribution of women.

MAHBUB UL HAQ

In speaking to you today, I will just make three quick points. First, as we review gender relations over the last few decades, it becomes very clear that it is a story of expanding capabilities and limited opportunities. In fact, when we look at education, health, and nutrition, in the last 20 years, women have covered ground that it took men three times as long to cover. The gender gaps, while they remain, have been more than halved over the last two decades. In primary and secondary enrollment and adult literacy in all regions of the world, including Arab regions, these gender gaps have been more than halved. And there are now 32 countries in the world where more women than men are enrolled at the tertiary level. In the last two decades, female life expectancy has increased twice as fast as that of males'; fertility rates have fallen by one-third; infant mortality rates have been more than halved; and one-half of couples in the world now use contraceptives compared to one-quarter only 20 years ago. Basically, this is a story of women expanding their capabilities fast and gaining control over their lives.

But there is still an unfinished agenda. Two-thirds of illiterates are women. Maternal mortality rates in the developing world are 35 times the rate in industrial countries. Fertility rates worldwide are still too high, with an average of 3.5. So while there is no question that there has been progress over the last two decades in reducing gender gaps and increasing capabilities, there is still some way to go.

And then we come to the second part of the equation: opportunities. Few economic or political doors are open to women. Seventy percent of the absolute poor are believed to be women. Women are concentrated in low-paying jobs and getting lower wages for equal work. Participation in the labor force has increased from 37 percent to 40 percent, only three percentage points, despite a doubling of female literacy in the last three decades. And when women do find jobs, their wage rate is less than 75 percent of the male wage rate. In some societies like Japan and Korea and the other industrializing tigers, the wage rate for women is less than half that of their male counterparts.

And what about credit? Less than 10 percent of the total world credit goes to women; in the multilateral institutions, less than 5 percent of credit goes to women.

In staffing? Globally, less than 15 percent of top managers and administrators are women; in the multilateral institutions, the average is even lower, with only 11 percent in senior positions in the U.N. system, World Bank, and regional development banks, and less than 8 percent in the International Monetary Fund. If you look at parliaments, less than 10 percent of parliaments are women; cabinets, less than 6 percent on average.

So it is clear that there are major constraints on economic and political participation. And one has to wonder why, despite expanding capabilities, there are such limited opportunities. The fight at Beijing and beyond is going to be to kick open those economic and political doors, while still continuing to reduce the gender gap in education and health.

In the United Nations Development Programme's (UNDP) *Human Development Report*, we have developed two indices—the gender development index (GDI) and the gender empowerment measure (GEM)—one to measure capabilities and the other to measure opportunities. The report shows how the countries of the world rank on these two indices and specifically where the problem areas are in each country.

The only real exception in the world is the Nordic countries. In Denmark, Finland, Norway, and Sweden, 40 percent of their parliaments are made up of women; in Sweden, 50 percent of its cabinet is made up of women. To achieve this level of participation, the Nordic countries fixed quotas in civil service, political parties, and cabinet positions. I realize that affirmative action is not too popular today, but when there are very entrenched power structures, the only way to make a change is through strong affirmative action. Whether it is a question of gender, poverty, or vulnerable groups, you do not shake up the power groups very easily unless there is a strong ally on your side.

My second point is that for a long time there has been a male conspiracy to keep women out of the national income accounts. For the first time, the UNDP has collected sample surveys from 80 countries stretching over the last two years on what work men and women do. And the conclusions are startling.

In the case of tradable work, which is work that can be done by a third person so that is can be traded and a value can be assigned to it, women worked 13 percent longer than men. (This is an underestimate because it does not count intensity of work, only the hours of work. For instance, women have made a habit of doing two or three jobs at the same time, such as cooking while looking after their children.) The national variations that you see in the report are very interesting. In Nordic countries, for example, there is not much of a gap. Men in the Nordic countries also do a good deal of work in the households and their communities, particularly because of changes in the social security legislation which gives them maternity leave for one year, and after that an option for another two years.

Although there are exceptions at the other end of the spectrum as well (for instance, in Italy it appears that women work 28 percent longer than men), the average of women working 13 percent longer than men holds fairly well in most countries, both developed and developing. The overall conclusions are inescapable: 1) women do most of the tradable work in the world; and 2) three-fourths of the work men do is in the market and only one-fourth is in the household or communities, while one-third of the work women do is in the market, and two-thirds is not paid. The result is that men get most of the income and recognition, whereas women, despite high contribution to the global output, still get much less of both.

Is there any reason we should not value the work of women? In 1926, Professor Pigon wrote: Isn't it strange that if a bachelor has hired a female housekeeper, her wages go into national income accounts. But the day that bachelor marries the housekeeper, national income falls, because she is now doing everything she was doing before plus more, but nobody takes account of it. In the latest UNDP report, we evaluate women's work in national income accounts—"the invisible contribution"—and it runs into trillions of dollars. What emerges is that women are the main breadwinners, globally and nationally, which effectively shakes up the conventional wisdom that women contribute very little to economic life.

But beyond just giving women's contributions a value, what is most important is the foundation on which gender relations in social and economic life are based. Why is it assumed that in property ownership, most of the property has been accumulated by the man just because he has been working in the market, even though women have contributed more to build up the property? Why is it that in the case of loans, women are regarded as uncreditworthy with no collateral, as if they are making no contribution to national income?

My third point involves the Beijing agenda. At least four priority actions need to be considered:

1) *Genderize the 20/20 Compact.* At the Social Summit in Copenhagen, both donors and developing countries endorsed the 20/20 Compact, which earmarks at least 20 percent of their budgets for direct attack on human deprivation by improving access to basic education, primary health care, family planning, and clean drinking water. Why not genderize 20/20 on the way from Copenhagen to Beijing? Because women suffer deprivation disproportionately (two-thirds of the world's poor are women), they should be given first claim on the 20/20—and not just the residual claim, as is often the case when budgets are cut, for instance, and female education gets cut instead of male education.

2) *Internationalize the Grameen Bank Project.* Credit is key to empowering women, yet we know that less than 10 percent of global credit—and less than 5 percent of multilateral credit—goes to women. According to survey after survey, 90 percent of food production in Africa is in the hands of women, and yet less than one percent of the world's

credit can be signed by them because men must sign for it, whether they work or not. By contrast, the Grameen Bank in Bangladesh gave over 90 percent of its credit to women in small unsubsidized loans, and women proved that they were the best investors and best savers, with a 98-percent recovery rate. What we need is an international Grameen Bank, and I was absolutely delighted when I saw last week that the World Bank, under its new leader James Wolfensohn, has decided to set up a $200-million window to support countries to have their own Grameen Banks, so as to get credit to the poor and particularly women.

3) *Commit to Legal Equality.* The Convention on Legal Equality passed easily, and in 1979 we all got excited about the Convention on Elimination of All Forms of Discrimination Against Women. But after 16 years, 90 countries either have not signed this convention, have not ratified it, or have entered reservations. And among those who have not ratified it is the United States. We need to pressure all countries to ratify the convention in the next five years. And even though it may take a long time to realize equality of rights in practice, this legal recognition is the first step in the process.

4) *Development Paradigms.* We have to go beyond the token women in development (WID) programs, which to my mind have been a disaster. Institution after institution, country after country, have set up WID programs. Normally, less than one percent of the total resources of institutions or governments go into WID programs. They are regarded as catalysts, but what we really need is to incorporate the gender dimension in *all* policies, in *all* programs, in *all* institutions. In the U.N. system, I do not believe we need the various institutions we have set up, from UNIFEM to INSTRAW to many others, with very diffused mandates, marginal resources, and very little contribution to education and health and other programs. What we need is an agency for advocating equality of women, women as agents of change, women as equal partners, equality under law, equality in development policy, credit systems, and opportunities. Under a woman of great eminence, perhaps with the stature of Gro Brundtland, such a policy agency would keep reminding the world that this must be at the top of the policy agenda in the twenty-first century, so that we do not have to meet only every ten years to remind the world that women are around. Can you imagine if there were no

UNICEF, whether there would be similar advocacy for children's issues? If there were no UNFPA, whether there would be a similar advocacy for population issues? We need these institutions as policy reminders, even though other institutions such as the World Bank are doing more for population in terms of funding than is the UNFPA. Why is it that we do not have a similar U.N. agency for women?

Let me conclude by just saying that unless women's issues are included in terms of policy and in terms of development program paradigms, just doing a few limited programs here and there is not going to open up the economic and political opportunities that are needed in the next phase. No society can ever progress, half liberated and half chained. Human development, if not engendered, is fatally endangered.

. . . .

THE ROLE OF THE MDBs IN IMPROVING THE STATUS OF WOMEN

MARGARET CATLEY-CARLSON

Today I want to talk about four things. First, why is it so difficult? Second, what do we really have to do about it? Third, how do the banks play a role? And fourth, how do we get there? And I hope I can help move people's minds to what really has to happen, because if I were to characterize the discussion so far, it is really still talking about the generic aspects of the problem: Women have a proven role; this role needs investment as much as—or more than—any other facet of international development; and not enough is being done. So let us try to concentrate on moving from the generic analysis of the problem to how multilateral development banks can be effective and good actors in that process.

First of all, why is this so difficult? It has been two decades since we realized that the development process did not really have it right—in other words, was not concentrating sufficiently on this area. That realization was initially almost intuitive, supported by what was going on in the West about women's roles and status, but increasingly buttressed by research and by good solid work. Why are we still in the situation where even to work on these issues may stigmatize somebody's career prospects within a financial institution?

At The Population Council, I think we have made a major contribution to understanding some of the reasons for the difficulty. We have put out something called *Families in Focus*, and it explores the myth of the family and the myth of how society really views many issues about the role of women and women's lives in an incorrect fashion. Take the myth of the family, for example. Every single political leader in every single country on earth gets up and says over and over again that the family is the bedrock of that particular society. Every single newspaper reporting on a good or a bad event traces back the family antecedents of the people in question. All of us know that the strength of the family is enormously important.

There are some myths about family that are widely accepted: The family is a stable unit; it has two parents attached to it; these parents have well-defined roles, father earns, mother nurtures; resources are shared equally in that family as a result of that partnership; and for some countries, families are multigenerational as well as stable. And even people who understand that the mythological picture may be changing still have the idea that this mythical image is where we ought to get back to.

Now, if you begin with that picture of a society, it is no wonder that an investment pattern starts to arise that privileges and favors a series of activities that will strengthen the picture.

But what is the *reality* of family today? They are smaller and they are nuclear. Even in a country like Egypt—where the myth about families is that they are multigenerational—72 percent of the families today are nuclear. This means that families are more vulnerable because there are less bits to hold it all together. They are also infinitely more transitory than was ever the case in the past.

Some of these changes are for traditional reasons. For example, widowhood is not decreasing, even with life expectancy increasing. Why? Because there is a built-in differential in age in marriage in many societies. And particularly for those societies that are now short of women, that differential will increase, and therefore widowhood is going to increase as well. You should not think of widowhood in terms of old women, but rather you should think of it in terms of young women with families, which leads to head of household status. There is also divorce and marital breakdown; the divorce rate in the United States is now 55 percent, and it is rising around the world so that the norm becomes 20–40 percent. There is movement of people for economic and environmental reasons, both of which are relatively new factors.

The result is that around the world single-headed households (which are about 3 percent male, 97 percent female) now make up about 30–35 percent of all households. This is an astonishing change, and it is very much a counter image to the "myth of the family." We have to start saying to our institutions that they need to look at the societies they are serving, look at who is being productive, and look at where the heads of the families are. If the endpoint of all development is to create units that work, children who go to school, and schools that are ready for the children, then we must look at what social factors are actually affecting the ability of that desirable endpoint to happen.

The family wage is deemed insufficient in most countries of the world except Japan. In other words, an average single wage earner cannot earn a family wage. That is the case in the United States, where 68 percent of women of even very young children are in the work force, and it is also the case in many traditional economies where mothers always worked but now also need to work in the cash economy in order to pay school fees and to have access to cash, which was perhaps not necessary before.

We are having later marriage in all societies—that is good for demographic forces. It is very good for the fact that women will be better equipped to play the role that I am describing to you and not the mythical role. Later marriage means more life experience, hopefully including a lot more school. We are also having fewer children per family. The per child norm has dropped from over 6 to just below 4 in the developing world, and a good bit lower if you take the whole world together.

The reality is also that resource distribution within families changes radically depending on who makes the money. This is not a new finding, but there is new research that underlines this more and more strongly. Between 90 and 100 percent of the resources that women earn go into the family, school fees, and health. The figure for men is around 70 percent and can be higher depending on the economy. The male contribution may be a larger overall amount, but it usually represents a smaller amount of his overall wage.

Now, what does this mean? It means that as policymakers are looking at what they consider to be the basic social unit of their societies—the family—they work from an operating myth that tells them they need to create a lot of jobs for men because the money coming in from the men will then be focused on children's school fees, health, etc. This, however, needs to be seriously examined on a country-by-country basis. Because if men's wages are not being channeled back into the family as is imagined, then this reality will serve to buttress the arguments that we need to make collectively about refocusing on women and the role women play within societies in order to achieve the desirable goals that all countries have as their national goals.

Women head more households than has ever before been the case, and they are more responsible economically within households. The economics of motherhood is changing, and there is nothing in the analysis that suggests this is going to change in the next two decades. Families are getting smaller; family dissolution is increasing all over the world. The family is more and more transitory, more and more nuclear, and so on. So we have some trends that should remain constant for at least the next while. We have to use these trends to make a compelling case for a different form of investment in women because of the different role that women are playing.

This is not startling news, because these trends have been evident for some time; in fact, this was all starting to happen a few decades ago. What we are now able to see is how concrete and how real these trends and tendencies are. Women have always been in a productive role vis-à-vis their families. The difference now is that their productive role in all economies translates into necessity for part of it to be in cash. Woman is now earner as well as nurturer.

Now what do we do about this? The first thing we have to do is seriously examine the male role. When we find out what is happening to families—that they are becoming more nuclear, more transitory—we need to take some serious looks at the father-child linkage and at fathering patterns. When you ask little girls around the world what they are going to be when they grow up, most of them say "mothers," and may add in various career goals. When you ask little boys what they are going to be when they grow up, fatherhood very rarely occurs on the list. This is something that leads to a potentially very difficult situation. We can take this on in our societies. I am not sure if the World Bank or the multilateral development banks are the best institutions to do it, or maybe I just have not thought of how I would get them to do it yet. But this is something we have to take on—the role of men in family and parenting.

The second thing that must happen is that we simply *must* make more investment in women. Women are already economic supports for the family, and the point is that they are not sufficiently strong in that role to be able to do it well enough. We must start changing that situation with wise investments in them.

What role do the multilateral banks play in this? There are the big three *P*'s for banks always—policies, programs, and projects. I think the policy role is undoubtedly the most important. We are moving into an era when bilateral development assistance is beginning to decline horrifically, significantly, and probably inevitably in most domains. The role of the multilateral development institutions is important now, and it is going to be vital in the future. The leadership that these institutions give on the policy level is going to be the single most important factor determining how leaders around the world look at what is happening within their own economies and societies. As seductive and tempting as programs and projects are, the energy must be focused on policy, because as big as multilateral development bank budgets are, they are minuscule compared to the aggregate of national budgets. And since the national budget is the target, the policy role of multilateral development institutions is the absolute key.

We have managed to draw a commendable amount of attention to the fact that there are a billion people in the world living on a dollar a day or less. Well, there are two billion people around the world that are living on $2 a day or less. What we now need to do, in a very clear-eyed fashion, is start doing the gender dissection of that two billion people and of those households. The more we look upon that in terms of households, the better we will be able to focus on what ought to happen.

The regional development banks and the World Bank have to spend a great deal of their policy effort talking about the kind of societies we want to create, in terms of numbers of children in school and productivity per household, and then talk about the instruments needed to get there. So policy is absolutely important.

I hope all of you have read the *Progress of Nations*, which is a UNICEF publication that sets out how countries are doing comparatively. The genius of this book is that it shows that at all levels of national income, it is possible to do better. It is too easy for finance ministers to hide behind poverty and behind lack of a resource base to explain why their countries cannot do as well in the social areas. The *Progress of Nations* says: "At this level of income, we would expect this many girls in school. Look at the countries that are doing better, and by the way look at the countries that are doing worse. At this level of income, we would expect this much child immunization. Look at the countries that are doing even better, and look at the countries who, with the same level of income, are doing worse." Get this book. Use it. It is your major policy tool, because if what we want to do is to say to every government on earth that you have policy options no matter what the level of national income is, then we have to show comparatively how other countries are doing better at all levels of national income.

We want to create a basic package of government measures that will include childhood immunization, at least four or five years of schooling for everybody, and a special focus on the under-served, who are usually poor and far too often female. Policy is national budget, policy is laws, policy is access—the access that different parts of society have to credit, land, property, and ownership. Those are the elements that we have to go after, continually, forcefully, unrelentingly.

The second *P* is program. We know which programs benefit women. We are getting better at these, and I think that the multilateral banks deserve at least part of the credit for that. Education, credit, and health are enormously important, and in the very good analysis coming out about the World Bank, they explain why, as do the UNDP report and others. At The Population Council, we spend a lot of time pulling out bullets for a sound-bite world of why education is important for girls. I will read you just a few:

- Women's wages rise by 10–20 percent for each year of schooling.

- Each year of maternal education is associated with a 5–10 percent decline in child mortality.

- One to three years of maternal schooling decreased child mortality by 15 percent; the same level of paternal education results in a 6 or 9 percent decrease. A study conducted in 13 African countries shows a

10 percent increase in female literacy leads to a 10-percent decline in infant mortality; male literacy has very little impact on infant mortality.

■ In terms of the next generation, in Pakistan, mother's education is the single strongest determinant for schooling the children in the next generation. Mother's education has a greater effect on children's education than father's, even though father's education has a greater effect on income.

The ammunition is there, but it needs to be used more effectively to draw people's feet back to the fire in the policy domain of why we must invest in these areas and what the impact will be on women.

The third *P*, projects, is important, so I would never belittle the WID projects. You have to start somewhere. They created a level of sensitivity and knowledge inter alia that this was not the way to go to make macro impact, but they also started creating an awareness that projects for women could on their own have some impact.

Population projects are important. There have been 20,000 children born since this meeting started, 5,000 of whom were not wanted by their parents. And perhaps more horrifyingly, several thousand abortions in the same time took place because of unwanted pregnancy and fertility. I do not think that women can control very much about their lives until they can control their fertility. And so, obviously, population projects are enormously important when we want to look at women and families.

However, I do have increasing problems with "small projects." We talk about women and then we immediately go to small projects. We have got one billion poor people in the world. We have got two billion people who are living in marginal or poor circumstances. How, in the twenty-first century, can multilateral development banks start talking about those phenomena in terms of their small project lending facility? This is the dominant problem on the earth and it has a very strong feminine aspect. I am glad that the small projects are there—I have seen how much they help—but if you take your first field of action as policy and your first need to focus the resources of the institute in this area, you do not come out with small projects.

Now, how to get there? The senior management role is absolutely key. Just as I think within these organizations the major and ultimate focus has to be on policy, I also think that within the organizations themselves the major focus of people who want to change this has to be in senior management. Guerrilla tactics, camp persuasion, shame—any possible weapon or mechanism can be used. Good policy research is important, but you also need to conduct a form of psychological warfare, I think, using good policy research. Until each and every senior manager is judged on his ability to understand, and until some of the managers are judged on her ability, we are not going to get anywhere.

The phrase around the East Coast—"they just don't get it"—is a very real phrase. And until the senior management of multilateral development institutions is judging his management team on whether or not they "get it," this is not going to happen. In particular, we want those very powerful policy and economic branches absolutely keyed in to making sure that these elements are brought in. So that has to be first and the rest will follow. It needs to be a subtle, sophisticated, guerrilla warfare campaign backed up by all the research, psychological pressure, etc., that can be mustered.

I believe in an efficiency rather than an equity case. You might pursue this issue because you personally believe in equity, but you will get further if you use the efficiency tools. Take the equity concerns and put them in your heart; take the efficiency tools and put them in your head. And then that will make a very powerful combination for improving the condition of the world's women.

SVEN SANDSTRÖM

I would like to organize my comments along three learning themes or perspectives from the World Bank's point of view. *First,* the more narrow perspective of how we are addressing women's and gender issues *per se* and how this has evolved—the sectoral perspective on which much of the discussion today has been focusing. *Second,* the broader country assistance perspective: How do women's issues relate to other aspects of our work and the overall development effort we are supporting? *Third,* a few words on our internal perspective—organization, staffing—and how that relates to women's and gender issues.

First, the sectoral perspective: Many years ago the Bank began with a focus on women as a "target" group of beneficiaries at the project level—particularly in education, health, and population projects. Over time, this evolved toward more of a sector policy focus in these areas. But what is very important is that there was a tremendous amount of research and evaluation work in parallel with these projects. And that helped us over time to demonstrate in a rather convincing way the high economic returns to society of investment in people, and particularly investment in women. Indeed, we like to say that investing in girls' education is probably the best investment in the developing world today. It is certainly a commonly accepted fact within the Bank—and is something that our staff is trying to follow through on.

This analysis and the demonstration of the broad impact of investing in girls and women is key for us in helping to convince government decision makers of the need to adjust priorities and to allow us to expand our support for these investments. It is largely a result of us being able to demonstrate these facts that we have been able to expand our lending for women and girls. This has been particularly striking in South Asia—for example, in Pakistan and India—and also in many parts of Africa.

It has been a very practical approach: learning by doing. We have combined projects with extensive evaluation and research in a systematic way, and we are now also using this approach to address women's issues in other sectoral areas—agriculture, credit, and more recently in infrastructure, particularly water and sanitation. We are also moving on to look at these issues in the context of labor markets, property rights, entry to trade, and services. In addition, we are beginning to look at the relationship between gender inequality and economic growth, and on the differential impact of economic reform programs on women and men. So the focus on the micro/macro, household/market linkages is increasing, and more and more research is being done in these areas.

Furthermore, our staff and managers are increasingly moving beyond these rather economic and technocratic types of analysis into a recognition of the role of women as key agents for change in society. Particularly in developing countries, we see the importance of women as leaders—in both business and politics—in effecting change toward more emphasis on poverty, equity, people, and the environment. In short, all the things that the World Bank is trying to promote. And this is increasingly driving our staff toward giving higher priority to supporting women and women's issues—and giving better balance between projects and policy.

In the paper which the Bank prepared for the Beijing Conference on Women, "Towards Gender Equality: The Role of Public Policy," we were trying to present the lessons we have learned, and how they can be translated into changes in public policy. Let me also just mention that this evolution from a rather narrow emphasis at the "micro" project level toward a broader policy approach is one that we have actually followed in many other sectors. It is particularly striking if you look at the analogy in the environment sector, where we started with fairly narrow reviews of environmental impacts of individual projects, but we are now doing research and evaluation of the linkages between macroeconomic policies and the environment. We are seeing the same kind of approach evolving in the area of women and gender issues. Again, it is a very practical "learning" approach, and it is one that enables us to work with client governments and other agencies to build up knowledge and understanding of these issues and the need for policy change. And over time, I believe it is the most effective way of getting change in the countries we are trying to help.

It is also very encouraging to see that we are doing more and more joint research on these issues with agencies that have much more expertise and experience than the Bank. For instance, we are collaborating with The Population Council on evaluation studies in a number of countries, including Ecuador, Ghana, and Vietnam. This learning approach might help explain why the Bank is sometimes perceived as being late with formal and ambitious policy statements. Our experience has been that policy statements must be grounded in experience and results in order to be effective and credible. I think it is fair to say that today there are more than enough grand policy statements and policy promises—but on the other hand there is a lack of results and, sometimes, credibility. So it is a question of getting the right balance and the right timing when you make these pronouncements. Similarly, there is a need to have the right balance between projects and policy. In the Bank, we cannot and should not focus solely on policy or on projects; it is the combination of the two that makes our work effective.

Turning to my second point, the overall country assistance perspective: We along with other development agencies have learned that there is no simple or single focus to the development challenge. It is important to recognize the complexity of development and the need to look at all sectors in an integrated way. The country itself has to make the assessment of the local situation, perceive the need for change, and plan the sequencing of this change.

We should remember that the Bank does *not* make the decisions on country priorities; it is the country and its people that ultimately make these decisions. Our role is to assist in the process, by sharing cross-country experience and research results and by working in partnership with the government and the people.

As a result of our learning, we are now giving much more emphasis to what we call the country assistance strategy, which is a framework for the strategy, priorities, and assistance program in each individual country. This country assistance strategy is the major focus of our work today, and it is clearly the area where women and gender issues should be fully integrated.

Part of the preparation of these country assistance strategies includes public expenditure reviews. In many ways, these reviews are a key instrument to effect change in investment priorities and to shift more investment into education, particularly of the education of girls, and other women's priorities, and away from subsidies of state-owned enterprises, military expenditures, etc. And public expenditure reviews are now receiving a much higher priority both in the Bank and the International Monetary Fund. Indeed, we are launching a research project in the Bank on public expenditure reviews and management to look at the experience so far and look at how we can make this tool even more effective.

It is also important in the country context to recognize that all donors and development institutions should not necessarily try to do everything in every country. It is much more effective to have some rational division of labor in each individual country or in each region depending on comparative advantages and strengths. To some extent, this explains why, in Latin America, for instance, the Inter-American Development Bank may have done more on women's and gender issues than the World Bank.

Finally, this leads to my third point: the internal perspective. The Bank, as is well known, is organized in a very decentralized way with the bulk of our staff concentrated in country departments—a structure that we introduced in 1987. This has led to major changes and improvements in the Bank's work program. Particularly striking has been the very dramatic increase in lending to the social sectors, which has increased five-fold since the organizational change.

We see the country departments and the staff as key agents to help catalyze change in the individual countries through the country assistance strategy tool mentioned earlier. The challenge here—which all multilateral development banks face—is to try to find the right balance between the country focus and the centralized technical expertise within the organization. Over time the focus may shift. In the case of the environment, for example, we started with a fairly large central technical staff but, over time, it has moved into the country departments. So we now have separate divisions in many areas dealing with the environment.

In the case of women and gender issues, we are focusing on not only the central role of research and policy dissemination, but also on training. It is very clear that to address gender issues, we need to get *all* staff in *all* sectors to pursue it. For example, the country economists may in many cases be more important as an agent of change than an individual technical expert on gender. It is this fundamental change in understanding—in attitude—that is really important and which we are giving attention.

And, finally, to effect this kind of change within our organization, we need more women not only in staff positions but more importantly in *management* positions. We have been able to expand the recruitment of women at the staff level very sharply over the last two or three years. In 1994, 40 percent of recruits at the higher professional staff level were women. The challenge now is how to get more women at the management levels—both through internal promotion and external recruitment.

ABOUT THE CONFERENCE PARTICIPANTS

NANCY BIRDSALL was appointed Executive Vice President of the Inter-American Development Bank (IDB) in 1993. Prior to joining the IDB she held various policy and management positions at the World Bank, including Director of the Policy Research Department, where she was responsible for economic policy and research on developing countries in such areas as public finance, trade, human resources, and macroeconomic policy. She chairs the Board of Directors of the International Center for Research on Women and is a member of the Board of The Population Council. Dr. Birdsall is the author of numerous publications on economic development issues, including education, health, population, labor markets, and the environment.

MAHBUB UL HAQ is currently President of the Human Development Center in Islamabad, Pakistan. From 1989–1995 he served as Special Advisor to the Administrator at the United Nations Development Programme. Previously, he was the Minister of Finance, Commerce, and Planning in Pakistan; Chief Economist of the Planning Commission in the Pakistani government; and Director of the Policy Planning Department at the World Bank. He founded the Third World Forum in 1973 and has served as Chairman of the North-South Roundtable (1979–1984), Eminent Advisor to the Brandt Commission (1980–82), and Governor of the International Monetary Fund (1985) and the World Bank (1988). He has published several books and articles on economic development, including *Sustainable Development: From Concept to Action* (UNCED, 1992) and *The UN System and the Bretton Woods Institutions* (Macmillan, 1995).

MARGARET CATLEY-CARLSON, President of The Population Council, is the first woman and the first non-American to head this international nonprofit organization. Previously, she was Deputy Minister of Health and Welfare in the Canadian government, President of the Canadian International Development Agency, and Deputy Executive Director (Operations) of UNICEF. Currently, she is the Chairperson of the Water Supply and Sanitation Collaborative Council and serves on the Board of Health of the Institute of Medicine of the National Academy of Sciences, as well as on the Boards of Appropriate Technology International, Women's World Banking, The Club of Rome, the Inter-American Dialogue, and the Overseas Development Council.

SVEN SANDSTRÖM was appointed Managing Director of the World Bank in 1991. He oversees the Bank's activities in Europe, Central Asia, and East Asia and the Pacific; the Bank's sector and operational policies; and the Bank's support for the International Development Association, the Global Environment Facility, and the Consultative Group for International Agricultural Research. Previously he held various management positions at the Bank, including Director of the Southern Africa Department (1987–1990) and Director of the Office of the President (1990–91). Prior to joining the Bank, he worked as a Research Associate at Massachusetts Institute of Technology and Harvard Business School.

About the Authors

MAYRA BUVINIĆ, President and founding member of the International Center for Research on Women (ICRW), is a social psychologist with extensive experience in the field of women in development. Dr. Buvinić is the author and editor of numerous publications on women and development, including "Projects for Women in the Third World: Explaining Their Misbehavior" (*World Development*, 1986); "The Fortunes of Adolescent Mothers and Their Children: A Study on the Transmission of Poverty in Santiago, Chile" (*Population and Development Review*, 1992); and "Targetting Female-Headed Households and Female-Maintained Families: Views on a Policy Dilemma" (*Economic Development and Cultural Change*, forthcoming). She most recently completed a research project on female-headed households and the reproduction of poverty in mother-daughter pairs. She is a member of the Board of Governors of the International Irrigation Management Institute (Sri Lanka), former President of the Association for Women in Development (Washington, DC), and past member of the Board of Trustees of the International Institute of Tropical Agriculture (Nigeria) and the Child Health Foundation (USA).

CATHERINE GWIN is Senior Vice President at ODC and directs ODC's international policy research program. Prior to joining ODC, she was Special Program Adviser to the Rockefeller Foundation, Senior Associate at the Carnegie Endowment for International Peace and Executive Director of the Council on Foreign Relation's 1980s Project. She is President of the African Economic Research Consortium and a director of numerous non-profit boards. She has written extensively on U.S. development cooperation policies and on the International Monetary Fund, World Bank, and other international economic and development institutions. Her publications include *U.S. Relations with the World Bank, 1945–92* (Brookings, 1994); and *Pulling Together: The International Monetary Fund in a Multipolar World* (ODC with Transaction Publishers, 1989). She also coauthored, with Albert Fishlow, Stephan Haggard, Dani Rodrik, and Robert Wade, *Miracle or Design? Lessons from the East Asian Experience* (ODC, 1994).

LISA M. BATES was formerly the Assistant Director of ODC's Population and Development Project and Research/Administrative Assistant to the Vice President for Studies of ODC. Before coming to ODC she worked for the Center for Women Policy Studies. She is currently pursuing graduate studies in public health and policy at Harvard University.

About the ODC

ODC is an international policy research institute based in Washington, D.C. that seeks to inform and improve the multilateral approaches and institutions—both global and regional—that will play increasingly important roles in the promotion of development and the management of related global problems.

ODC's program of multilateral analysis and dialogue is designed to explore ideas and approaches for enhancing global cooperation, to build networks of new leadership among public and private actors around the world, and to inform decisionmaking on selected development topics of broad international concern.

ODC is private, nonprofit organization funded by foundations, corporations, governments, and private individuals.

Stephen J. Friedman is the Chairman of the Overseas Development Council, and the Council's President is John W. Sewell.

ODC
1875 Connecticut Avenue, NW
Suite 1012
Washington, DC 20009
(202) 234-8701

ODC Board of Directors

About the ICRW

The International Center for Research on Women (ICRW) is dedicated to promoting development with women's full participation. ICRW works in collaboration with policymakers, researchers, and practitioners throughout Africa, Asia, and Latin America to address the economic, social, and health status of women in developing countries.

ICRW is engaged in policy-oriented research, program support and analysis services, and an active communications program. ICRW's focus is on economic policies, such as the effects of structural adjustment on women's employment and their access to credit and other resources; on the formation and dynamics of family and household structures; on women's health and nutrition as these relate to their roles as economic producers, nurturers, and health care providers for their families; and on the links between women and environmental degradation and protection.

ICRW is a private, nonprofit organization that is supported by grants, contracts, and contributions from international and national development agencies, foundations, corporations, and individuals. Established in 1976, ICRW has its offices in Washington, DC.

ICRW
1717 Massachusetts Avenue, NW
Suite 302
Washington, DC 20036
(202) 797-0007

ICRW Board of Directors